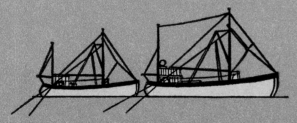

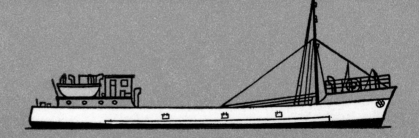

To the Memory of Wolfgang Steinitz

Wolfgang Rudolph

Boats–Rafts–Ships

VAN NOSTRAND
REINHOLD COMPANY
New York Cincinnati Toronto
London Melbourne

Van Nostrand Reinhold Company Regional Offices:
New York Cincinnati Chicago Millbrae Dallas

Van Nostrand Reinhold Company International Offices:
London Toronto Melbourne

Copyright © 1974 by Edition Leipzig
Library of Congress Catalog Card Number 73-16832
ISBN 0-442-27186-7

Translated from the German by T. Lux Feininger
Design by Walter Schiller
Text illustrations by Ludwig Winkler
Produced by Offizin Andersen Nexö, Leipzig

Printed in ~~the German Democratic Republic~~ Germany (East)
Published by Van Nostrand Reinhold Company
A Division of Litton Educational Publishing, Inc.
450 West 33rd Street, New York N.Y. 10001

16 15 14 13 12 11 10 9 8 7 6 5 4 3 2 1

Ill. p. 2: Cargo vessel of Lake Geneva (after Cecil Trew).
Ill. p. 3: Chinese five-masted junk of Woosung (after Warrington Smyth).

Contents 5

6

Rocket-powered space automatons, guided by remote control towards Moon, Mars, Venus and Jupiter, symbolize in our time the peak of scientific and technological achievement of transportation. Between them and all other means of communication exists a large gap. Its immensity is nowhere else more evident than in the field of waterborne traffic. On the high seas, on rivers and on lakes, the presence of rafts and sailing vessels, of paddle-propelled dugouts and kayaks, is to this hour an everyday occurrence. According to statistics more than a million sailing vessels and oar-driven boats are in use at the present time, carrying cargoes, or serving in the fisheries and in local passenger transport. Nor are such vehicles used as working tools only; hundreds of thousands of persons live continually on and in waterborne vessels of the most diverse kind. Throughout the world, ships and floating hulls continue to be connected with living folkways and cultic ceremonials in many ways. In Calcutta, Rangoon, Singapore, Bangkok, Canton and Shanghai, on the east coast of Africa, in the delta of the Euphrates and Tigris, on the Amazon, in Greenland, Alaska and Tierra del Fuego, but equally in Finnmarken, in the Spreewald, at the mouth of the Rhine, Meuse and Schelde, in the Aegean Sea, this life may be observed. Maritime traffic in the 20th century is not exclusively determined by airfoil boats and hydroplanes, nor by mammoth tankers, container ships, gas turbines, nuclear power plants, electronic control or satellite navigation. Whoever assumes this, would be mistaking a part of our civilization for the whole.

For this reason we consider it to be both useful and necessary to draw attention to the "simple forms" of water craft and to depict the peculiarities of various modes of living.

Collective life aboard ships is marked by characteristics quite different from everyday life on shore. As in older times, the seafaring population constitutes today a special community of distinctive coloring effecting manifold and intense cultural exchanges.

For almost a century, serious ethnographers have engaged in research on maritime cultures and modes of living. Although the impetus was given by Englishmen—Seligman, Malinowski, Radcliffe-Brown, Haddon, Firth—and by Scandinavians, such as Erixon, Itkonen, Granlund and Birket-Smith—there are outstanding scholars also in many other countries: Frobenius, Boas, Nishimura, the team of the Hamburg South Seas Expedition, Te Rangi Hiroa, Heine-Geldern, Gusinde, Leopold Schmidt. Stimulated by these as well as self-motivated, countless professional colleagues have made significant contributions—not to forget the prominent researchers or laymen belonging to other disciplines: Heyerdahl, Paris, Piétri, Worcester, White, Suder, Chapelle and Crone. Particularly valuable help has come from representatives of archeology and philology. Organized maritime studies were the program of the British Society for Nautical Research, founded in 1910. Shortly after World War One, the systematic ethnographical survey of folk types of small craft was begun, Szymanski in Germany and Hornell in the British Colonial Empire being the originators. But within the last decade some specialists have dedicated themselves totally to the investigation of maritime cultural history: Hasslöf, Henningsen, Crumlin, Cederlund, Christensen, Rudolph, Greenhill, Prins, van Beylen, Fraser, Anderson. The time is ripe for a first summing up of cultural-historical data.

8

In our presentation of forms and functions of vessels we shall proceed from the basis of considering the life of those directly involved in fishing and navigation, the workers represented by the seafaring and fishing populations of the various global cultures. We shall examine the evolution of water traffic in conjunction with the distinctive environmental conditions and successive cultural-historical situations. In this, we shall emphasize older forms and stages, for the reason that they are commonly the least known. We shall seek examples among the more typical conditions, but also underscore special developments. We should like to give preferential attention to the cultural achievements of seafaring populations outside of Europe, as well as to the contribution made by the presently all but forgotten marginal maritime civilizations of Europe. The goal is, to clarify the course of developments and processes without regard to continental or national boundaries.

In the concluding chapter we present examples of specific professional qualities of the life of 19th century seamen and fishermen. Conditioned by our sources of knowledge, we find ourselves restricted to a consideration of the pertinent situations in northern Europe. On the east coast of the United States and Canada they were more or less identical, as also, probably, in southern Europe. On the other hand the life rhythms of the fishing and seafaring populations of most of the southern, Indian and Pacific oceanic areas require further intense and thorough study. Here and there we shall enlarge the field of vision to merge into the present. We shall, however, confine ourselves to occasional hints at features of transition, the history of modern highly industrialized navigation not being the subject of our studies.

Scratch drawing of a Bidjugo boat, part of a mural painting on the wall of a house on the Bissagos island Urakan off Guinea-Bissau (after Hugo Adolf Bernatzik).

Right:
Raft from Peru made of coupled pumpkin shells, 16th century (after Theodor de Bry).

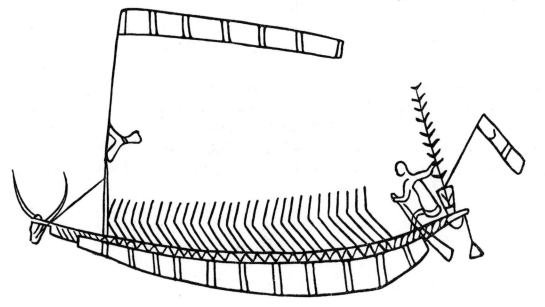

Original Forms of Water Craft

The Beginnings of Navigation

For the earliest prehistorical period of human society, the old stone age, the probable use of boatlike vessels on the waters of the warmer zones may be assumed. On the other hand, the inhospitable climate of wide regions bordering the ice-age glacier rims will hardly have offered much enticement for water voyages to the hunters and gatherers of the period. The making and use of water craft may well have begun with those tribal communities whose life patterns centered on fishing, the hunting of water game, and shore-side gathering, who had consequently attained a high degree of familiarity with their aqueous habitat and who had also become settled to some extent. Groups of such specialized gatherers or "littoral small-game hunters" have been identified as existing from the transition of the later old stone age to the middle stone age onward, crudely simplified as the period between the 9th and 10th millennium, and in Southeast Asia, Uganda and on the shores of the Caspian Sea; later in the Mediterranean area and in the region north of the Black Sea, lastly also in northern Europe between the Atlantic Ocean and the Baltic, and in Japan.

Ideal conditions for such a way of life were found on the banks of large rivers, on the shores of lakes, deltas, lagoons and shallow ocean bays. The sea and the forest offered a balanced variety of animal and vegetable food in the form of fruit-bearing and tuberous plants, herbs and wild honey, fishes, clams, crabs, turtles, seals, porpoises, birds' eggs and game. In the tropical regions, the inhabitants of fishing camps would have found an abundance of bamboo, a giant grass susceptible of being worked even without the help of ground stone tools, and of the most variable uses. Other useful raw materials for the making of simple water craft for trips to outlying reefs or nearby islets would be various types of rushes, sedges and reeds, as well as the fruit of tropical gourd-bearing plants, for the fashioning of which clam shells and splinters of quartz would be sufficient. Next to the tropics, it is probable that the temperate latitudes—whether in the deltas and lagoons of the Mediterranean and the Black Sea, or in the bays of the Baltic or even of the Atlantic—offered in those times similarly favorable conditions. As a matter of fact, the oldest archeological indications of boatlike vessels belonging to fishing and beach-gathering civilizations occur in northern Europe during the 8th millennium. Future excavations, in particular outside Europe, may bring us closer to an eventual clarification of the problem of the archeological development of water craft, which is part of the larger problem of the archeology of civilization. As regards chronology, we should be further advanced if we were able to date exactly the beginnings of the settling of such islands as the Andamans, Celebes, Borneo and certain of the Philippines, for these parts of the world were probably accessible to early stone age man only by sea.

The first step in the ethnographical examination of ship-like vehicles is an exact description of their various aspects, beginning logically with their shape and ways of manufacturing; next, a consideration of the traditions of life on board, the various uses the vessel may be put to: whether as a working tool or habitation. Lastly, it is of importance to learn about the valuation put on the respective vessels by their owners. On this depends the ornamentation of vessels, their distinction by means of symbols, their names and the rites connected with their uses in folkways and cults. Finally, the ethnographer finds of interest pictures where ships are the theme of artistic presentation.

The material thus collected requires systematic ordering. For the purpose of classifying the manufacturing modes of water craft we examine them in terms of the formal principles of native local boatbuilding. Early man created his water vehicles in three fundamental types of technology which, though divisible in dozens of variations, are determined by different local conditions and cultural traditions. From his earliest experiences with swimming aids—driftwood, fagots of rushes, inflated skins—primitive man developed the effective coupling of naturally floating materials, as well as of hollow containers artificially made capable of floating. The results of this kind of "colligative technology" were various types of rafts.

Another category of manufacturing, utilizing the principle of shell fabrication, produced single-unit, hollow vessels capable of bearing loads. Representatives of this category are found wherever primeval forests offered an inexhaustible supply of massive timber. The principle results in the "subtractive technique": the volume of a baulk of timber is reduced by means of preparatory burning or charring, and subsequent chip-removal effecting a hollowing. This was the origin of the dugout type of craft. Other builders utilized the "deformative technique", which, although belonging to the same category of shell fabrication, proceeds by transforming plastic, i.e. flexible and pliable materials, without altering their volume. This produces pod-shaped hollow vessels made of tree bark, or ceramic containers resembling the husks or shells of nuts or fruit.

A third technological category, created by still other types of civilization, leads to the production of water craft according to the frame principle. Multiple-unit vessels consist of a form-giving framework or skeleton and a covering outer skin. Boats of this kind owe their being neither to the reduction of volume nor to the transformation of materials, but are commonly built, in accordance with the "constructive technique". Of the several manufacturing principles, this was alone to prove capable of evolution, but it became possible only after wooden planks were used for the covering of the skeletal shape.

Rafts

The distribution of rafts as a species of water craft is world-wide. There are but few waters on which there was not made, at one time or another, at least occasional experimentation with the colligation of naturally floating bodies. Nevertheless, there are clearly recognizable focal points of distribution for the several kinds of rafts: areas in which rafts continue to be in fairly common use to the present day.

The following regions show the occurrence of floats or rafts made of tree logs (ill. 3) or ligneous bamboo stalks: the coasts of the Indian subcontinent and the Southeast Asian waters between the Mekong delta and Taiwan; New Guinea and the Melanesian islands; lastly, Ecuador, Peru and Brazil. In methods of joining the logs together we distinguish between the generally more common lashings and the technique of fastening by means of dowels, which is confined to relatively few areas. The dowels, or treenails, made of hardwood, may join all the parts together, or they may be used to link only two logs of a layer. Besides these types, another variation of logwood raft is known, whose components are not only longitudinally trimmed and joined, but are subsequently shaped by way of chip removal. We are speaking of the East Indian catamarans, the central longitudinal sections of which are shaped as stem and stern, while the outer logs are fashioned to function as gunwales. The bow is given a wedgelike, pointed shape.

Rafts composed of more or less thickly bunched fascines of a variety of stout stalks of grasses or grass-like herbaceous plants and shrubs (rushes, sedges, papyrus), fagots of branches of the cotton plant, limbs of the corklike sola tree, as well as palm leaf fiber and palm leaf stalks, have been made in nearly all the watery regions of the tropical, subtropical and temperate zones. The best documented occurrences come from North and Central Africa, i.e.

from Morocco and the Nile region to Lake Chad, and from the west coast of South America, from Mexico as far inland as Lake Titicaca in the High Andes (ill. 4). The aboriginal peoples of Tasmania and New Caledonia made rafts of strips of tree bark tied in bundles (ill. 1). Such vessels vary in shape from simple platforms made of from two to three bundles of equal thickness, to complicated structures composed of from four to six bundles of varied thickness with raised gunwales. The ends are frequently bent up vertically in skilfully tapered points.

Within the group of raft types consisting of joined solids that have been made floatable artificially, we recognize a concentration of the occurrence of inflated skin rafts in the region extending from Armenia and Arabia to Mongolia, as well as to the upper reaches of the Indus, Ganges, Hoang-Ho and Yangtze rivers. An isolated instance occurred formerly on the Chilean coast (ill. 2). In the Middle East, the skins of sheep, goats, yaks and buffaloes were adapted for use as floats, while in Chile sealskins were used. The orifices of the floats pointed upward, so as to permit inflation, if necessary, during the trip, by means of a reed or hollow bone. Depending on the usage the raft was to be put to, three, four or more, up to 1600 skin floats were fastened together, onto which understructure gridlike platforms of tree branches, saplings, or baulks of timber might be attached. Lastly, we find types of rafts consisting either of coupled ceramic vessels, or of coupled and emptied fruit husks, of spherical or bottle-shaped gourds. Pottery jugs, the mouths of which were closed by stoppers made of waxed leaves, fastened together in rows of three, were preponderantly employed on the sandy shoals of Indian rivers. Two areas of distribution of gourd rafts are known: one in Central and South America, the other in the Sudan, between Niger and the Nile.

Propulsion of rafts is commonly by means of poling or paddling. Sail power was in use on wooden rafts in India, Vietnam, Taiwan, on the Polynesian Mangareva islands, along the Andean coast of South America and in Brazil. Rafts made of fascines of rushes and fitted with sails are in use in our time on Lake Titicaca (ill. 5). We assume the existence of similar types for the early civilizations of Egypt, Mesopotamia and the Indus region. The antiquity of most raft types is documented, partly by artistic representations, such as reliefs of Pharaonic papyrus rafts on the Nile and of Assyrian skin rafts on the Euphrates, and partly by popular terms and references dating back thousands of years.

1 Raft made of bunches of eucalyptus bark on the coast of Tasmania. From: François Péron, Voyage aux terres australes, Paris 1824, 2nd ed.

Discussion of the use of rafts opens up very interesting problems. Let us first look at the social aspect of this question. Dieter Schori has pointed out that several specific references designate rafts in Oceania to be the water craft of the poorer strata of the population, chiefly as the working tool of fishermen. Around 1880, the price of a hog on New Britain in Melanesia was ten strings of clamshell money,

A. Plan d'une Balse faite de peaux de loup marin cousus à pleine d'air.
B. Indien sur une Balse vûe de Cote. C. autre vûe de front
D. Traverses pour rassembler les deux moitiez de la balse E. trou pour l'enfler et la remplir d'air. F. maniere de Coudre les peaux
G. Loup marin à terre H. Pinguin.

2 *Inflated skin raft made of sealskin, from the Changos on the north coast of Chile.*
From: M. Frézier, Relation du voyage de la mer du Sud, Paris 1732.

while the fee for building a boat was at least twice this amount. Whoever was unable to raise the funds was compelled to make his own raft for fishing.

We are indebted to Walter Ivens for giving valuable indications on the use of rafts on a cult basis. On the Melanesian island Malaita of the Solomon Group, the womenfolk of the Lau fishing population were compelled to dwell in isolated huts during their period of menstruation, and to procure their own necessities. The use of canoes was forbidden; a vessel thus polluted would have been burnt by the men. In order to obtain drinking water and food, the women made rafts for themselves. The same taboo prohibiting the use of boats applied to the periods preceding and following confinement.

Even children have their own rafts, and not only in Oceania. On many other coasts children continue to our day to make floats for themselves out of bundles of sedges, etc., often evincing much skill in this summer amusement.

Economically speaking, rafts are used principally as fishing vessels and as ferries, but have also been employed in cargo services, e.g. on the Andean coast of South America and in Mesopotamia; in Oceania, specifically for the transporting of heavy cargoes for the building of cultic structures, such as the megalithic tombs. Depending on the requirements of the trip to be made, cargo rafts may be fitted with cooking hearths, covered dwellings and special cargo containers. Rafts of all types, whether made for fishing or for cargos, are characterized by minimal draught and great elasticity, which is of advantage in surf and in the passage of rapids. Aside from work uses, rafts continue in our time to be used as supports for permanent dwellings, for instance in the Amazon region, where in Belem and Manaus, entire fishing suburbs of raft-houses are in existence; likewise in Southeast Asia and southern China,

"The inflated skins were closed with stoppers and arranged in a square on the water, forming a raft a meter long on the side. In the middle it consisted of nothing but water, to be sure. Is this supposed to be the seat? Wait, now why did they bring these branches? They were laid crosswise on top of the watery square. Beneath and beside me everything was bobbling and slopping. It is not very comfortable to sit on criss-crossing tree branches. One of the skins had something un-animal-like about it: it had been patched ... Although I was launched on the river, I was still close to the shore. The current tried to sweep me along; at the water's edge five men were holding the raft by two ropes, which they tied to the horse. One of them jumped on the bare back of the beast and forced the unwilling animal into the water; at the same time, two other men jumped into the river. The waves seized us. A glance at the two fellows who stayed ashore showed me that we were hurtling downriver, at what I estimated to be about 35 kilometers an hour. The horse was hitched to this foursome, itself imbedded in three of the larger belt-floats made of goatskins. Jerking his head anxiously above the fierce waves, the horse strained directly toward the opposite shore. The two men were floating on the port side in the water, acting as human steering oars; hanging on to my seat by their hands, they made frog-like motions with their feet only. ...At last the horseman seized some reeds, although he had to let go again because the current drove us onward. But we had received a good push forward; soon two of us could hold on to some more reeds. The Amu-Darja tugged fiercely. But it was too late; the horse's feet were on the ground. We waded ashore. The horse was tied to a shrub, the goatskins were hauled ashore. The swimmers shook themselves, the water flying about; we went tiger hunting."

Egon Erwin Kisch:
Asien gründlich verändert, 1932
(Asia thoroughly changed)

"Others are made to carry Goods: the Bottom of these is made of 20 or 30 great Trees of about 20, 30 or 40 Foot long... pinn'd fast to each other, and then pinn'd to the undermost Row: this double Row of Planks makes the bottom of the Float... From this bottom the Raft is raised to about 10 foot higher, with rows of Posts sometimes set upright, and supporting a floor or two... The lowest of these Stories serves as a Cellar: there they lay great Stones for Ballast, and their Jars for fresh Water... The second story is for the Seamen and their Necessaries. Above this second Story the Goods are stowed, to what height they please, usually about 8 or 10 feet, and kept together by Poles set upright quite round: only there is a little space abaft for the Steers-men, (for they have a large Rudder) and afore for the Fire-hearth, to dress their Victuals, especially when they make long voyages, as from *Lima* to *Truxillo*, or *Guiaquil*, or *Panama*, which last Voyage is 5 or 600 leagues. In the midst of all, among the Goods, rises a Mast, to which is fasten'd a large Sail... These Rafts carry 60 or 70 Tuns of Good and upwards; their Cargo is chiefly Wine, Oil, Flour, Sugar, *Quito* cloth, Soap, Goat-skins drest, &c. The Float is manag'd usually by 3 or 4 Men..."

William Dampier:
A New Voyage Round the World,
1697
(Dover Publ., Inc., N. Y.)

where we find kitchen and flower gardens, even small fields, on rafts. In the thirties of our century, 90 "floating villages" *(thuy co)* with about 33,000 inhabitants were counted in the delta of the Red River in Vietnam (ill. 158). The question is often asked, whether there is a historical progression from raft to boat, and whether it is correct to view rafts as the general forerunners of ships. To this one may at least say that there is no doubt that the type of log raft fashioned by chip removal constitutes a possibility for development into shoal-draught, flat-bottomed boats, because a boat bottom constructed of a few planks can be thought of as deriving just as readily from the dividing of a log or bark shell as from a permanent joining of catamaran-like raft sections.

3 Small log rafts (Jangada), on carts for transport across the wide, level sandy beach; they are used to gather seaweed for fertilizer on the northern Portuguese coast.

4 Uro fishermen of Lake Titicaca (Peru) making a raft
of bundles of reed.

Right:
5 Rafts made of fascines of reed from Lake Titicaca (Peru).

6 *Indians of Guiana building
a bark shell boat.
From: Jules Crevaux, Voyages dans
l'Amérique du Sud, Paris 1883.*

7 *An Algonkian Indian from Canada making preparations for building a birchbark boat, 1965.*

8 Fishing dugouts decorated with colorful
ornaments of the Senegal coast.

9 In the Amazon basin, dugout canoes,
which are also used by children,
are today still the indispensable means
of transportation and communication
of the Indian forest people.

10 *Kayak from Greenland.*

11 *Umiak of the Greenland Eskimos, about 1900.*

12 *Circular frame boat on a river in southern India.*

Boat shells made through chip removal resulting in shape changes—dugouts or log canoes—are to be seen in the museums of all countries. They are also still in use, not merely in western Canada, on the Amazon or in the African primeval forests (ill. 8, 9), but in Europe, for instance with the Polish fishermen of the Narew. The last log boat of the lower Oder was broken up in 1925. At the Mondsee in upper Austria a dugout was built as recently as 1967. The building technique has remained virtually unchanged since the earliest times: fire was used for felling the tree as well as for the preparatory charring of the log core (ill. 13). Afterwards, the hollowing process continued with broadaxe and adze. On very primitive levels, clamshell scrapers seem to have sufficed. This sounds simple, but let us remember what a mass of experientially gained knowledge of the forest and its various woods, transmitted from one generation to the other, is necessary merely to decide on the best season of the year for cutting trees, on the various types of soil, mountain slopes, exposure to weather, etc. What skill is required, for example, to carry out the controlled method of volume reduction, frequently encountered, whereby holes are drilled into the log from the outside. As soon as the hollowing process reaches the drilled gauge from within, the hole is plugged tight. This may seem like an obvious solution, but first, somebody had to invent it.

Nor should we forget that the making of dugouts was just one branch of woodworking in the primitive civilizations, and that there was a close connection between it and many other ways of using wood in related techniques: the carving of watering and baking troughs, butcher's tubs, drinking vessels, scoops and winnowing shovels, mortars, beehives, shoulder yokes and bowl-shaped carrying containers. Other related processes are wood splitting techniques, used in the making of baskets, splitwood pouches, mats and fish traps, and the hewing of blocks, beams and boards by means of broadaxe and adze. Georg Friederici has enumerated seven timber species used in North America for the cutting of ship shells: pine, white fir, cedar, tulip, chestnut, walnut and oak. Almost all lengths had their uses: we know of log canoes barely 3 meters long, but also, at the other extreme, of vessels such as Columbus measured in Jamaica, of a length of 30 meters and a breadth of 2.50 meters.

Propulsion of dugout canoes was either by poling or by the thrust of a freely held oar used from a standing, kneeling or sitting position, for which in the last century the originally English term of "paddling" has become internationally familiar. The largest log vessels of the Antilles, the Amazon, the Congo and the Canadian northwest coast had crews of from 80 to 100 paddlers.

26

13 *Making a log canoe in Virginia, on the east coast of North America.*
From: Theodor de Bry, Collectiones peregrinatorium in Indiam, Frankfurt 1590.

Next to their worldwide distribution, the multifarious uses to which log vessels have been put on the most varied kinds of waters should be underscored. They were to be found on ponds and tarns, on creeks and ditches no wider than a yard, on lakes, rivers and ocean bays. Lengthy sea voyages seem to have been made in log boats on the Baltic, and also between Florida and the Bahamas.

Special mention is due the log canoes in which some North American Indian tribes gathered harvests of wild rice. Neither should the role of log canoes as objects of barter be forgotten. Lastly we may note the periodic use of dugout canoes on land, whether as containers for the making of fish oil, as oil presses, or as a kind of giant winemaking bowl for festive ceremonials; boats capable of holding as much as 2000 liters have been used for this.

In four major forest regions of the globe, single-unit shell boats were made by the deformative process from the plastic material of tree bark. These zones are, firstly, southeastern Africa between Lake Tanganyika, Zambezi and Okavango; secondly, in Australia and in the interior of some of the Indonesian islands. The third region is the lands settled by the Ewenks (Tungus), north of the Amur and east of the Yenisei rivers; the fourth, the American areas of the broad belt of woodlands extending from Alaska to the New England states in the north, and Guiana and Brazil in the south (ill. 6, 7).

In Australia, James Hornell was able to examine almost all possible formal variations of single-unit treebark boats, from very simple trough-shaped vessels in the southeast, whose open ends were caulked with lumps of clay, to beautiful and entirely seaworthy boats, 12 meters long, in the building of which a steaming process had been used to make pliable the bark at the boat's ends. All these hulls had the bracing and stiffening lateral and longitudinal framework fitted—where it was used at all—after completion of the outer shell. Single tree branches, bundles of stout twigs, naturally bent timber knees either singly or bound together in pairs, as well as thwarts were used. Bark boats of this kind were employed only in the fisheries and for ferrying. They were driven by poling or paddling. The Australians in the Gulf of Carpentaria went as far as 20 miles offshore in them.

Ceramically made boat shells might be dismissed as insignificant curiosities, if we did not know that the use of the *tigari* in the Ganges delta has been documented since ancient times. They are hemispherical vessels, shaped on the potter's wheel, of barely 1 meter diameter and approximately 40 cm depth. They have always been the water transport of the poorest of the village population, who used them during the periodic inundations, in house-to-house traffic, and to go to the market. Dozens of such shells used to be seen near schools, being the means of conveyance of the school children. The rider sat on a hay bundle or on a piece of board; going upriver the children would paddle a perfectly straight course, and downstream they let the current gyrate their vessel as it would. On village feast days in Bengal there were even tigari regattas. Ceramic boat shells resembling the Indian ones were used in ancient times also in the valley of the Nile. Round or oval boat shells made of plaited bamboo mats—often without crosswise stiffened interior wooden braces—are used in Vietnam.

14 Relief showing a circular frame boat, from the palace of the Assyrian king Sennacherib at Nineveh, about 690 B.C.

Hollow containers capable of floating may be built with a frame covered by an outer skin. Such vehicles may be constructed with pointed ends as well as on a circular plan (ill. 12). Accordingly, some scholars distinguish in this class between a round type and boatlike vessels. Between the two extremes the most diverse intermediate forms are to be found: bathtub shaped, ovoid and rectangular boats, all built on the same structural principle. The materials for frames were ligneous grasses (bamboo), wood (willow, hazel, birch, juniper, ash, poplar, pine) or animal bones. In some places the frame was erected with the keel uppermost, in others with the aperture pointing upwards. For the outer skins, materials such as the hides of goats or cattle, bear or seal skins, but also closely woven fabrics of plant stalks were used. Tannin, tree resin and animal tallow were used to preserve the structure. In Mesopotamia, the boat's skin was indued with bituminous asphalt. All joining of the component parts was done by sewing or lashing. An archaic division of labor was observed in the construction of Eskimo vessels, where the men made the framework, and the women made the boat covering.

Framed boats in the 18th and 19th centuries were distributed over a large contiguous region comprising northeastern Siberia, Alaska, Canada and Greenland. Ireland, Scotland and Wales also belonged to this northern zone. In the 17th century, skin-covered framed boats were made by the Lapps in northern Scandinavia and by the Finnish-Ugrian tribes of northern Russia.

In the southern zone, we find small areas of occurrence in Central Africa, also in the river region of Euphrates and Tigris, in Turkmenistan and Usbekistan, in Tibet, the Persian Gulf and southern India, and in Polynesia. The American areas were the prairies of the Midwest on both banks of the Missouri and the Tennessee rivers and the lower Colorado region in the north, and the steppes of Venezuela, through Bolivia to Patagonia, in the southern section of the continent. Zones of occurrence of boatbuilding technologies cannot be simply equated with population group types. For the most distant antiquity, say the late old stone age, such equations may apply. But for the more recent epochs we know that this kind of identification is erroneous. For example, tribes of the Algonkian Indians have made skin-covered frame vessels as well as bark shell types, and in Wales log canoes were in simultaneous use with frame boats.

Most frame boats are certainly of great typological age. For Mesopotamian craft this is documented by relief representations from the Assyrian royal palaces of Nineveh, which date to the 8th century B.C. The term *quppu* for "boat" already appears in the 3rd millennium B.C. in Akkadian cuneiform inscriptions, and we need not be in doubt that the vessel thus designated is identical with the *guffa* of today (ill. 14).

Some of these prototypes were of respectable dimensions. In Mesopotamia and southern India there were round basket boats of 5 meters diameter. The travelling craft of the Eskimos, the umiak, was up to 20 meters long (ill. 11). They were propelled by single and double paddles, and square sails made of the guts of seals were set from a yard on the boats of the Bering Sea. In conclusion, brief mention must be made of the vessels of the Polynesian Chatham Islands, which are located 400 nautical miles east of New Zealand. The Moriori—a peace-loving people exterminated in the 19th century—made these boats with a tub-shaped wooden frame, the interstices of which were closed by the intertwining of a web made of the cork-like floral stems of an insular species of iris.

"The single-seat Baidare is to these people what the horse is to the Cossack. This vehicle is a narrow, long floating bladder made of seal skins, pointed in front, stretched out over a light wooden skeleton. In the middle is a round opening: the man sits inside with feet stretched straight before him, his torso projecting above the covering. He is joined to the floating vehicle by a hose made of Kamlaika fabric, which fits closely about the aperture at one end, the other being laced around the body beneath the arms. Grasping his light oar in his hands, his weapons laid in front of him, holding his balance like a horseman, he skims over the water like an arrow."

Adalbert von Chamisso:
Reise um die Welt,
1821 (Journey Around the World)

The remaining crevices were stopped up by braiding in fern stalks and seaweed. They were clearly frame boats and not rafts, as some scientists have thought, even though water may have penetrated the web. These vessels were described in 1791, the date of the first arrival of Europeans, as being driven by means of rowing, from a sitting or standing position, and also by sculling. Stone hearths were fitted for seal hunting expeditions, and on such occasions the boats might go up to 20 miles offshore.

Generally speaking, the prototypes of frame boats were made and used for fishing and the hunting of water game. Even today, in the age of space flight, the kayak of Greenland confronts us as a boat of the highest perfection and the utmost seaworthiness (ill. 10). But frame boats were also used as cargo carriers, e.g. in Mesopotamia. From the point of view of cultural-historical significance, their role as river ferries on the Tibetan-Chinese tea caravan routes and pilgrimage highways is not to be underestimated.

"The big, or women's boat, in Greenland language the Umiak, is commonly six fathoms long, or it might be as much as eight or nine, about four to five feet wide, about three feet deep, pointed fore and aft, and flat below. It is composed of light battens or rods, joined together with whalebone and covered with seal leather...

For this work the Greenlander has neither chalkline nor square, but still he knows how to shape it to the proper proportion by eye alone. All his tools are a small keyhole saw, a chisel which serves him for a hatchet, a small auger and a pocket knife ground to a point. After he has finished the wooden skeleton, the woman covers it with newly tanned, thick seal leather which is still white, and caulks the seams with old blubber; treated in this way, these boats leak far less than wooden ones, because the seams swell tight in the water. The boats are rowed by the womenfolk, of whom there are commonly four, with another one steering aft with an oar. In these boats they travel with their tents, all their household goods and other belongings, and frequently with between ten and twenty passengers, from one place to another, a hundred or two hundred miles. The men travel alongside in their kayaks, with which they protect the Umiak from the big waves, in an emergency keeping it on an even keel through seizing hold of the gunwale with their hands. They commonly travel about six miles a day in such a boat."

David Crantz:
Historie von Grönland, (History of Greenland)
1765

Innovations in Construction

The dimensions of all single-unit ship shells are subject to natural limitations. The length and thickness of a single tree trunk cannot be exceeded, and tree bark cannot be made to assume all the shapes that may be desired. Recognition of this fact led, thousands of years ago, to a significant achievement of invention which has remained nameless: very thin-walled log shells were boiled in liquids with addition of animal fats and albuminous substances, or special mixtures of mineral oils, which softened the shell sufficiently to allow it to be extended by pull and pressure, and to insert bracing and stiffening elements: the ribs (ill. 19). This produced broader vessels, capable of supporting greater deadweight.

Three areas of distribution of log hull extension are recognizable in the 19th century: a northern Eurasian one, from Finland to Kamchatka (which in earlier times,

as a find of a wreck in Bornholm indicates, may have reached an even more westerly limit), a second one on the northwest American coast of Alaska and Canada, and a third one in India and Southeast Asia.

A general advance in development demanded qualitative changes, which were accomplished through considering the new construction technique at the time of fashioning the shell. Formal suggestions for this procedure may have been received from the contemplation of containers no longer made from a single hollowed block, but which had begun to be composed of several parts as soon as the art of shaping boards out of tree logs was understood. This new process led to actual shipbuilding; to be sure, not everywhere at the same time, and with a broad variety of transitional stages. At least two avenues of technical progress lead from the dugout to the planked boat. Firstly, the prototype may be heightened, broadened and lengthened by fitting strakes and planks, which results in the so-called bottom shell boat (ill.15). Secondly, a hull shell—whether log type or bark slab type—may be faithfully copied by means of piecing together separate sections.

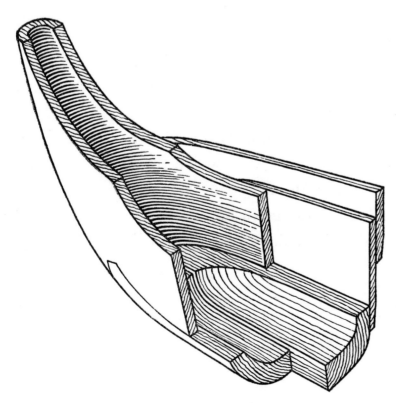

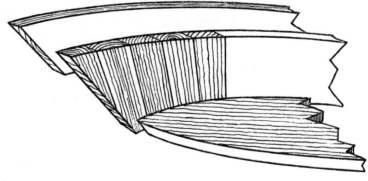

15 At left: Hollowed block stem of a bottom shell boat from Lake Sommen in Småland, Sweden (after Albert Nilsson).
At right: Vertical carvel planking of fore and after ends of the boats of the Cassubian fishermen of Lake Leba in Pomerania (after Kurt Kühn).

The three-part or five-part plank or bark slab types of boats deriving from such methods likewise overcome the limitations posed by the prototype. Tree log rafts likewise may have induced the idea of making boat hulls by means of permanent joining of the component parts.

All multiple-unit boat hulls necessitate joining of the structural elements. Two methods were developed for the plank strake type, which from the technical angle is the most important: the planks were set one above the other on their narrow sides, or with their broad sides overlapping in the manner of roof tiles. This produced a smooth (carvel) or stepped (clinker) hull side. Flush-laid planks were joined together by means of sewing, dowelling or trunnelling, or spiking; clinker-laid planks were fastened by sewing or nailing (ill. 16).

The idea of broadening and heightening a dugout by means of fitting planks to the body was probably conceived independently in different parts of the world. Areas of distribution in the 18th and 19th centuries were widely scattered: we find them in the Alps, in the east of Europe between the Baltic, the White and Caspian Seas, in the Indian subcontinent and in all of Southeast Asia (ill. 17), thence radiating into Polynesia; lastly in Japan. In Africa, bottom shell boats are encountered in a region forming a belt reaching from Guinea to the great lakes of Uganda. In America, two areas of distribution are recognizable: the Alaskan and Canadian northwest coast, and the Caribbean Sea. It is certain that local, individual inventions as well as influences from the outside were responsible for this mixed pattern.

16 Different types of side-plank fastening:

Carvel planking
                                                           Clinker planking

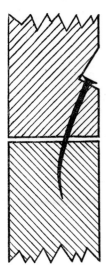  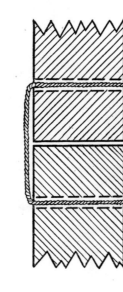 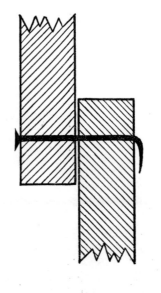 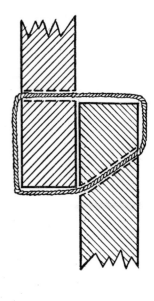

nailed or spiked   *doweled or treenailed*   *sewn*   *riveted*   *sewn*

The origins of the more highly developed shell construction with planks appear to be of a different order. The oldest examples of this type are documented from the 3rd millennium and belong to the bronze age civilizations of the region bounded by Egypt, the Aegean countries, Mesopotamia and the valley of the Indus. In less distant

17 Boat dwelling of the Moken, a tribe of littoral small game hunters and beach gatherers in the Burmese Mergui Archipelago of Southeast Asia (after Walter White).

These vessels are bottom shell boats, built on top of an expanded log canoe which forms the base. The topsides are made of tied palmleaf stalks, the roof-shaped cover is made of palm leaves.

The families of the orang laut (water people), as these coastal nomads are called, wander in groups of 10 to 30 boats from one island to the next. Their children are brought up entirely in the boats and they also eat and sleep in them, leaving them only for the purpose of food-gathering. Even during the rainy season of the stormy monsoon they live for the most part in the beached vessels. The men spear fishes, catch turtles, hunt wild pigs and gather coconuts and birds' eggs. The women and children collect crabs, clams and algae in the shoal water and the coral reefs, and fruit, herbs and wild honey on the outskirts of the mangrove jungle. In their existence the barter trade with the Burmese and Malayan settlers on the coast plays an important part.

18 Boat of the Indians of Tierra del Fuego. From: Narrative of the Surveying Voyages of "Adventure" and "Beagle", Vol. II, London 1839.

Already Forster and Darwin had observed the uncommonly archaic work organization on the basis of division of labor according to sex of the Indians of Tierra del Fuego. More recently, Gusinde explored deeply the civilization and mode of living of these sub-antarctic littoral hunters. His studies have dispelled several false conceptions, e.g. as regards their boatbuilding. The water craft of these people, which are quite indispensable to their way of life, cannot be qualified in the least as "primitive". They are multiple-unit, sewn beech-bark canoes, stiffened with inserted ribs and stabilized by means of a layer of loam distributed over the entire bottom surface. Gusinde described them as "masterpieces of optimal functionalism, a supreme achievement of the technology of these Indians". They were built collectively by the men, but once in commission, were cared for and paddled by women exclusively. Before departing from the beach, husband and wife of the Yamana family discussed and agreed on the course to be steered, and the destination of the trip. During the daily hunting excursions, each family member had its regular place in the boat. The man squatted in the bow in constant readiness for any game that might be sighted; in the waist, the children watched over the fire on the open hearth; astern, the wife, or mother and daughter, paddled. Only the most precisely attuned interaction between both partners assured success at hunting whatever game might be encountered on the way—whether seal, otter, or seabirds. Over the course of years the couples attained a high degree of perfection in their collaboration. Marriage, among the Yamana, had the meaning of entering consciously into a working partnership; the spouses enjoyed perfect equality of rights.

times, we encounter planked ship construction in northern Europe and in the regions of the Far Eastern old bronze age civilizations of northern China and Southeast Asia, with traces extending into Melanesia. When the striking coincidence of two important structural characteristics, i.e. shell construction and planks fastened by treenails, is considered, the assumption of an ancient, common origin of the technique in the Pontic–Asia Minor area gains much in probability.

Despite much fruitful research, the early developmental history of American multi-unit bark boats continues to pose several riddles (ill. 26). The dwellers in the northern forest belt between Alaska and New England, the Indian tribes belonging to the Athapaskan and Algonkian linguistic groups, clearly built in accordance with the principle of shell construction. Nevertheless, the technical perfection of their use of interior wooden braces is such as to make a very early influence by frame construction methods a possibility. This method had begun to be practiced somewhat earlier by their southern prairie neighbors, chiefly by tribes belonging to the Sioux group. After the immigration of the Eskimos, the method reached utmost perfection also in the North. It cannot be viewed as surprising that the frequent and far-reaching migrations of all these fishing and hunting tribes should have led to contacts resulting in an interchange of experiences in the fabrication of vitally essential transport craft.

Another unexplained factor is the history of evolution of multiple-unit shell boats in Tierra del Fuego. Here the Alakaluf and Yamana, two non-sedentary Indian fishing and beach-gathering tribes, constructed their vessels by means of sewing long slabs of bark together (ill. 18). For the time being, the manufacturing of multiple-unit boat shells in Vietnam remains likewise unexplained; these shells are made of a framework of bamboo and plaited bamboo mats and may be as much as 20 meters long. The several stages of the building technique resemble those of bark boats. A noteworthy factor is the curing of the mat shell by means of application of a mixture of resin, palm oil and cattle dung, to which special earths are added.

The ocean area between India and Southeast Asia was the point of departure for yet another kind of innovation, the fitting of outriggers to sailing log canoes and bottom shell boats, for the purpose of increasing stability (ill. 22). Outriggers were probably developed in different ways in the various coastal regions: on the one hand, bundles of slender bamboo poles lashed parallel to the boat side, on the other, powerful balancing beams, which were lashed athwart the middle section of the boat, projecting outwards and ballasted, depending on the strength of the wind, by one, two or three men of the crew. Both original types are still to be met in our time. Stabilizers parallel to the longitudinal axis occur on the turbulent rapids of the upper Mekong in Laos and on the Irrawaddy, as well as on other rivers in Burma; stabilizers of the transverse type are used in the Vietnamese coastal waters, on the Indian Coromandel coast, in Ceylon and in the region of the mouth of the Indus.

19 Building an expanded log canoe in Bengal, 1969.

20 Max Pechstein (1881–1955): The Return of the Wherries at Nidden. Oil painting, 1912.
The wherries (Keitelkähne) of the Courlandian fishermen of the Kuržiu Neringa (Courland peninsula) were carvel-built shell boats. Next to their construction and rig, the most noteworthy features of these vessels built by migrant boat or wherry-builders were the carved weather vanes and the open cooking hearths in the after part of the vessel.

Right:
21 Maurice Seghers (1883–1959): Otter on the Schelde River. Drawing (undated).
The graphic work of this Antwerp artist forms the concluding chapter of the nautical iconography of the Schelde–Meuse–Rhine region begun by Pieter Breughel the Elder. Seghers made a great many drawings in the tradition of a Nooms and a LeComte, of sailing vessels of all kinds. In the course of many years this work grew into an inventory of high quality, documenting not so much accidental scenes as stressing the typical appearance of each type of vessel of the period around 1900. The otter was a Belgian type of cargo carrier.

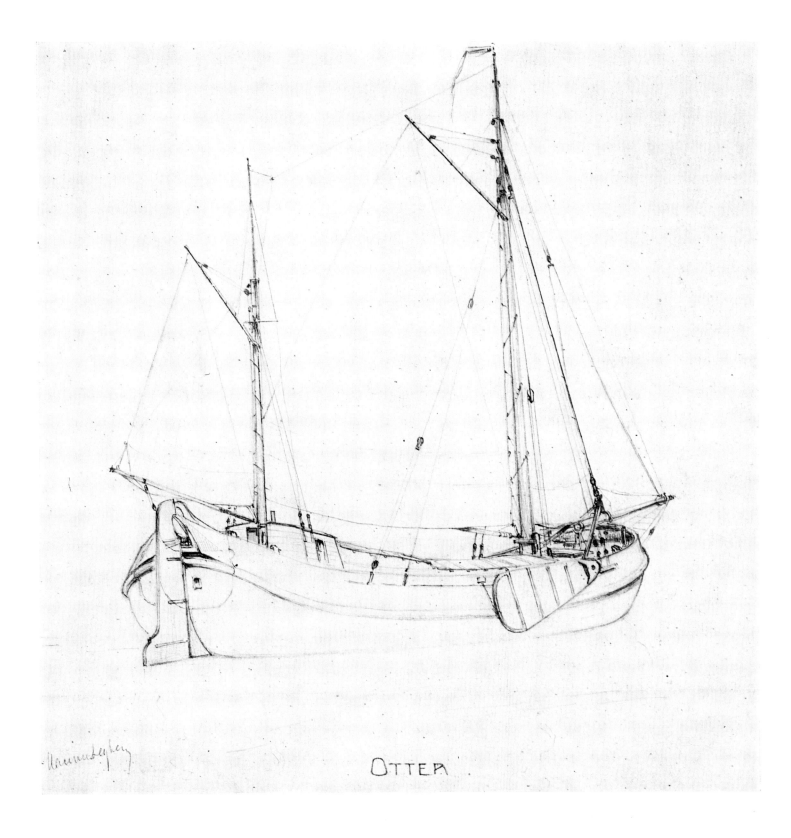

OTTER.

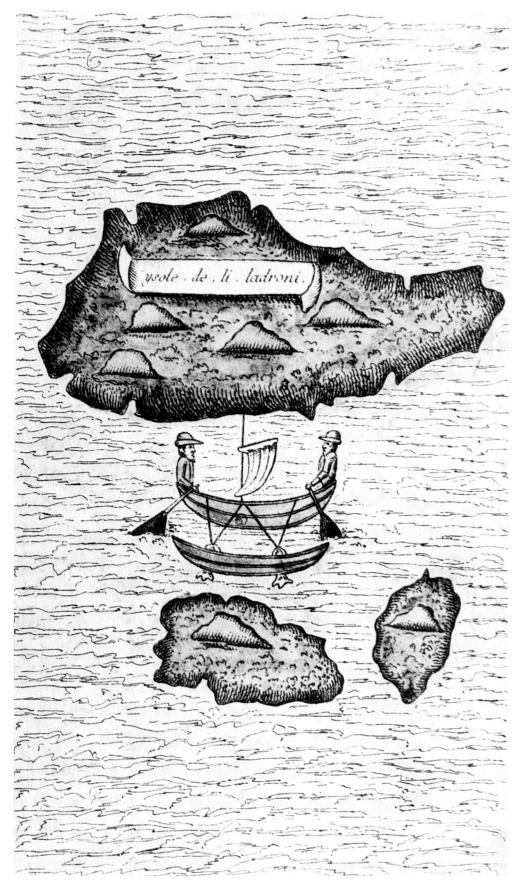

ysole . de . li . ladroni .

22 *The oldest European illustration of an outrigger vessel from the Marianas Islands, Micronesia, published in Pigafetta's Journal of the Circumnavigation of the World with Magellan (1519 to 1522).*
From: Antonio Pigafetta, Premier voyage autour du monde sur l'escadre de Magellan, Paris 1799.

Right:
23 *Outrigger boat with sails from the Santa Cruz Islands, Melanesia, in the Museum für Völkerkunde, West Berlin.*

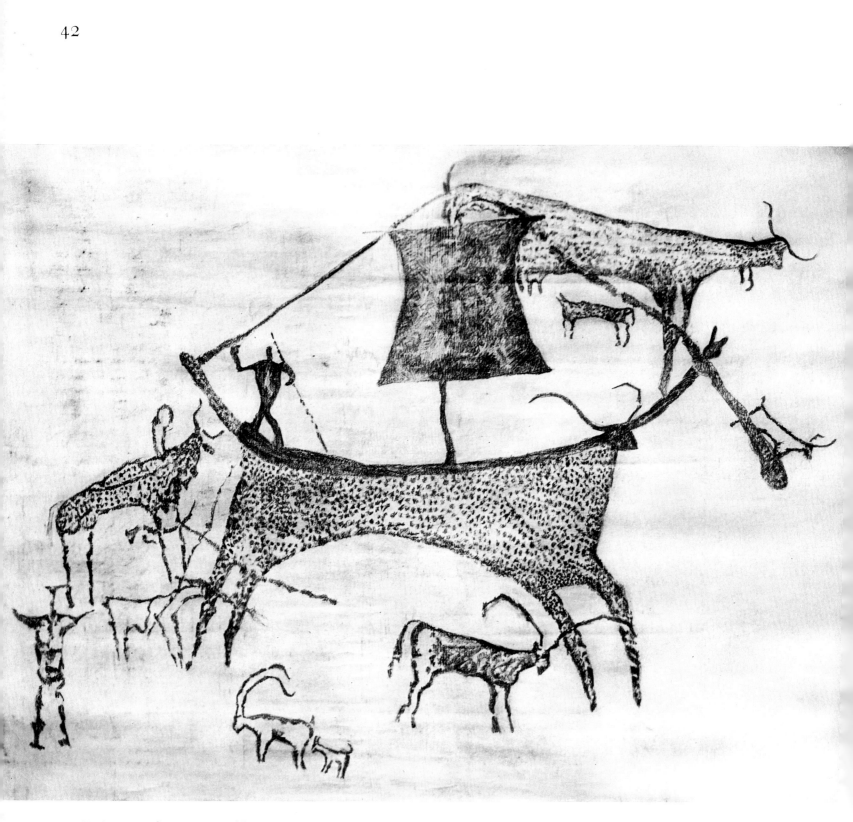

24 Rock mural of a sailing-ship (?) at Wadi Hodein Magoll, Nubia, about 6th to 4th millennium B. C.

25 The Vazimba fishermen of the west coast of Madagascar use one-sided outrigger dugouts with a very old-fashioned rig.

A quadrangular sail is rigged, depending on the wind direction and on the course, either parallel or at right angles to the longitudinal axis by means of fan-wise diverging spreaders.

26 *Algonkian Indian from Canada sewing together the birchbark skin of a canoe.*

Beginning with the dark ages of prehistoric and early historic times, technical inventions by sailors and fishermen regarding the modes of propulsion of their craft have taken place. In river travel the natural force of the current was often all that was necessary. Examples of this we see in the last remaining, non-motorized barges on central European rivers, where even today the most primitive manpower is used: the thrust of the poling stake against the river bottom. Water traffic requiring steering, on the other hand, demands a better mode of propulsion, even on rivers and landlocked lakes, e.g. by means of unsupported oars, or paddles. This is done from a standing,

27 *Tree branches as an improvised sail on an Indian dugout canoe in Guiana.*
From: Jules Crevaux, Voyages dans l'Amérique du Sud, Paris 1883.

kneeling or sitting position and the oarsman is facing forward on his course. Special regional variants of lightweight, hand-held oars were poling oars with a fork-shaped attachment at the blade base, and double-bladed paddles.

The first documentation of a revolutionizing innovation in propulsion comes from Egypt and Mesopotamia around the year 2500 B.C. This is the rowing oar or sweep, pivoted on the gunwale, the oar being actuated from a standing or sitting position while facing astern (ill. 36). The technique of the pulling oar presupposes, on the one hand, familiarity with the physical law of leverage; on the other, it seems to express an indication of a shift in social conditions. It confirms the presence of the principle of the division of labor, which is of such significance in the history of civilization, inasmuch as we encounter here the juxtaposition of the rowing crew and the steersman. This alone need not yet imply a fundamental change in the structure of the boat's crew; however, the time and place of this revolution suggest that the invention of the ship rowed with sweeps belongs to the epoch of early class society. This is not the same as stating that the rowing crews must generally have been slaves: there may have been partnership crews of free shipmen. Nonetheless it is certain that the Mesopotamian and Egyptian rulers despatched a goodly portion of the most vigorous of their prisoners of war to serve on the river and ocean ships of their respective states as slaves.

At present, the oldest known proof of the use of pivoting oars in northern Europe is the Nydam boat (400 B.C.) from Schleswig. The Mainz tombstone of the Rhenish-Celtic sailor Blusses from the middle of the first century A.D. is the earliest central European finding, whereas a golden boat model from North Ireland gives evidence of the use of oars about A.D. 50.

Originally perhaps less striking, although destined eventually to reach far greater significance than the invention of rowing, was the introduction of sails. In certain

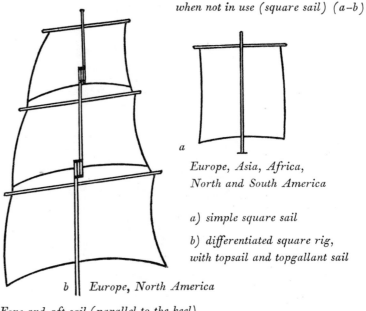

28 *Principal forms of sails* — *Sails rigged at right angles to the keel when not in use (square sail) (a–b)*

a

Europe, Asia, Africa, North and South America

a) simple square sail

b) differentiated square rig, with topsail and topgallant sail

b *Europe, North America*

Fore-and-aft sail (parallel to the keel)
1. extending forward of the mast as well as abaft (c-f)

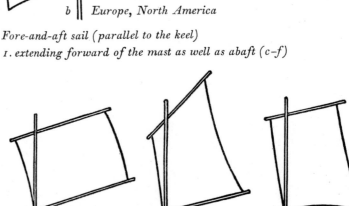

c   *c*   *c*

India, Indonesia, Melanesia   *Southeast Asia*   *Europe*

c) quadrangular with tack fastened to mast (standing lug)

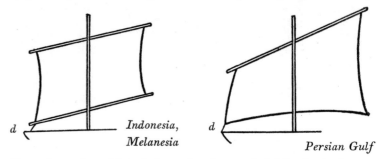

d   *Indonesia,*   *d*
           Melanesia   *Persian Gulf*

d) quadrangular with tack fastened to bow or deck (dipping lug)

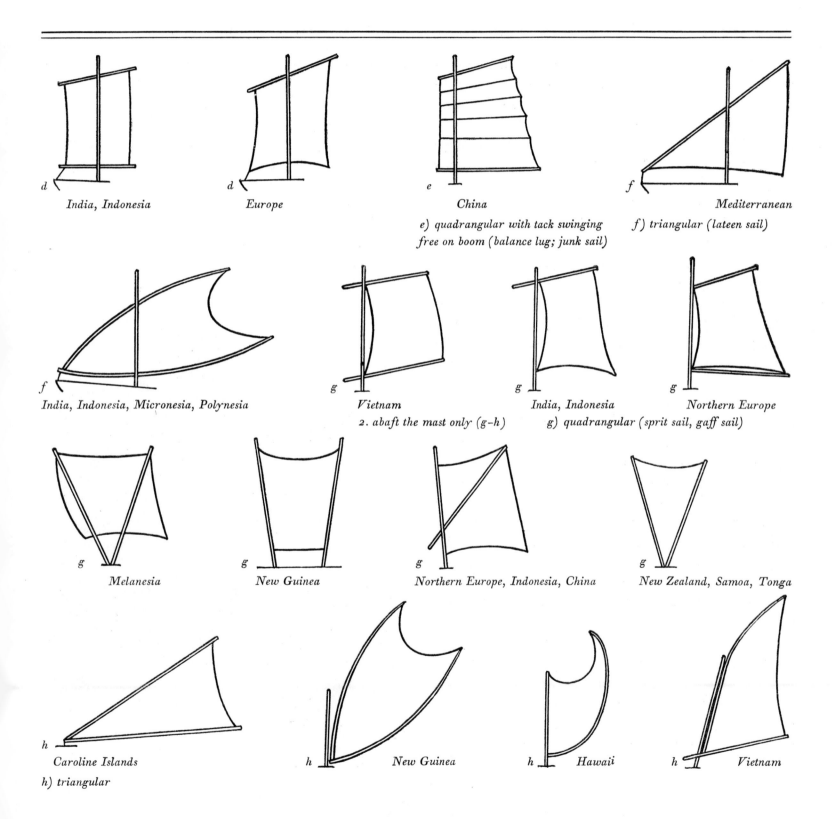

d   India, Indonesia

d   Europe

e   China

f   Mediterranean

*e) quadrangular with tack swinging
free on boom (balance lug; junk sail)*

f) triangular (lateen sail)

f   India, Indonesia, Micronesia, Polynesia

g   Vietnam

g   India, Indonesia

g   Northern Europe

2. abaft the mast only (g–h)

g) quadrangular (sprit sail, gaff sail)

g   Melanesia

g   New Guinea

g   Northern Europe, Indonesia, China

g   New Zealand, Samoa, Tonga

h   Caroline Islands

h   New Guinea

h   Hawaii

h   Vietnam

h) triangular

localities sailing is surely of very ancient origin. Approximately coeval occurrences in Mesopotamia and Egypt are documented for the turn of the 4th to the 3rd millennium. Artistic representations of sailing craft from Crete and the civilizations of the Indus region date back to more recent times. It was only with the arrival of sailpower that a cargo-carrying sea trade became a possibility, even though perhaps originally depending on a leading wind. There is no doubt that locally and chronologically independent initial stages of development led to the oldest known type of rig, which shows a square sail spread transversely across the longitudinal axis of the ship by means of a spar, the yard (ill. 24). The prototypes of sails of which we have proof were made of flattened and stretched animal skins or guts, also bunches of brushwood placed in the bow of the boat, as well as spread mats woven of bamboo fiber, rushes or palm leaves (ill. 27). This kind of equipment was still to be found in manifold use in the 20th century. Square-rigged navigation may be due to indigenous invention, or it may constitute a loan development, depending on the type of civilization.

Free steering oars, handled either singly or in pairs from the stern, were already known at the period of the larger, paddle-propelled boats of the ancient civilizations between Nile and Indus. For sailing they were absolutely indispensable, and underwent an improvement, inasmuch as they were suspended in a sling, which formed an elastic joint with the upper planks of the stern (ill. 29). The ages-old daggerboards of sailing rafts have a function similar to the rudders of sailboats. When the Europeans of the period between 1450 and 1600 in their groping progress toward new continents in their heavy square-riggers reached the distant shores, they noted with amazement the high state of development of steering by means of daggerboards. This happened in East India and on the coast between Vietnam and northern China, as

well as off Ecuador, Peru and Brazil. The sailors of the Far East employed daggerboards not only for steering their sailing rafts but also in boats and ships, in order to lessen lateral drifting due to wind action. We do not know just when leeboards and daggerboards made their first appearance in small craft on the coasts of the North Sea and the Baltic. The oldest pictorial representations from the Netherlands are dated about 1570 and indicate some kind of connection with the gradual transition from the square rig to new types of sail plans.

29 Helmsman of a large sailing outrigger boat of New Guinea.

Early Mediterranean Civilizations

The Eastern Civilizations

Ancient American and African Empires

Northern European Navigation

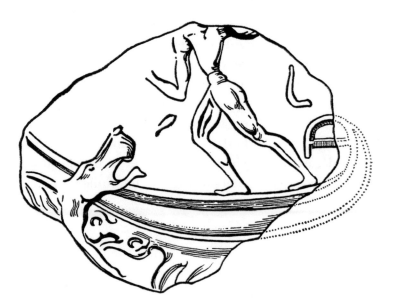

EARLY MEDITERRANEAN CIVILIZATIONS

Egypt

The existence of fisheries and local water traffic with rafts or boats in the Mediterranean, soon after the beginnings of settlement near the coast, need not be demonstrated. The estuaries and deltas of the big rivers Ebro, Rhone, Po and Nile constituted ideal grounds for such a development, and the islands of the Aegean and Adriatic seas must necessarily have enticed the coastal dwellers to their first offshore trips. During the 5th millennium, advances due to the metal age, which was reaching a respectable degree of progress on the eastern Mediterranean shore, especially among that culture connected with agriculture and bronze metallurgy, ushered in a "Golden Age" of Mediterranean navigation in response to the need for improved means of ore transportation over long sea distances. Artifacts originating from this ocean commerce, such as tools, household wares, weapons, ornaments and cultic objects, very considerably helped to modify the lives of individuals as well as the existence of entire societies. With the bronze age, ocean navigation entered the field of human awareness for good. Henceforth it forms part of the repertoire of existential modes of being.

Where formerly some few representations of vessels in scratched incisions on vases from Syros, an island in the Aegean Cyclades, most vaguely and tentatively dated about 2500 B.C., were regarded as the earliest evidence of Mediterranean navigation, the most recent archeological reports allow the assignment of much earlier origins to the beginnings of organized Mediterranean seafaring. The oldest city-like harbors on the Syrian and Lebanese coast—Ugarit and Byblos—are thought to belong to the period of colored ceramics of the late 6th millennium.

In Egypt the construction of planked boats alongside the traditional manufacturing of papyrus rafts is demonstrable for the transition period from the 4th to the 3rd millennium. These represent a revolutionizing qualitative technical innovation, even if it did not originate in the valley of the Nile, which probability seems almost a certainty. The evolution of Mediterranean Near Eastern shipbuilding continues to present many riddles. It is established that as early as the 4th millennium there was lively navigatory activity on the Nile, this being essential for the existence of the inhabitants of the alluvial tracts. The entire mode of being of these people was stamped by the river, a water highway without any alternative. There can be no doubt that the settled planters made rafts of papyrus bundles, surrounded as they were by an abundance of the raw material; elsewhere, possibly, boats were also made from bark slabs sewn or laced together. We know of rafts made of fascines of papyrus, rushes or corkwood branches, from pictorial representations of the Pharaonic period; to this day they are found in the upper Sudan, in Ethiopia and on the Central African Lake Chad—but also in Sardinia in the Mediterranean. In 1969 and 1970 Thor Heyerdahl proved by the experiment of his two bold "Ra" voyages, that such rafts can be made in large dimensions, able to carry considerable deadweight, and that they can be sailed; they are capable of making sea voyages of more than 3000 miles (ill. 33). It would thus have been perfectly possible for the early traders of the bronze age civilization to employ papyrus rafts for the sea transport of crude ore, and perhaps they actually did so. The Isis myth, according to which the sorrowing goddess went in quest of the corpse of her husband Osiris on a papyrus raft, shows that in ancient Egypt vessels of this type served not only in agricultural and commercial pursuits, but were also cultic objects.

Illustration page 49:
Seal stone of Crete with motif from a sailor legend, around 2000 B.C.
(after August Köster).

The question of how plank boats of the traditional shape of papyrus rafts came to be built in the swamplands of the Nile, which are poor in timber, cannot at present be answered. In the beginning, this new type of water craft seems to have served in the observances of cults rather than in an economic role. All we can state at this time is that—from the beginning of a certain level of civilization, the so-called Negade 2 period, tentatively dated around 3000 B.C., evidently contemporary with far-reaching changes in the entire social structure: the transition from a classless to a class society—there were two types of water craft in the valley of the Nile; peasants and fishermen must have used papyrus rafts, while the raft-shaped plank boats were the privilege of the ruling class. It is likely that wooden shipbuilding in old Egypt—not from imported Lebanon cedar, but using native acacia, mulberry and ficus timber—was to benefit the working people only many generations later.

30 Ancient Egyptian boat-carrying procession during the Water Feast in the second month of the inundation of the Nile. This representation from the 14th century B.C. is part of the great frieze in the Temple of Luxor.
From: Walther Wolf, Das schöne Fest von Opet, Leipzig 1931.

In 1970, the first complete report of the significant discovery of the Cheops ship was published. This is the oldest wooden water craft known to exist in the world today, ascribed to the period about 2500 B.C. Investigations of the air and watertight funeral chambers south of the great pyramid of Cheops in May 1954, had revealed that in one of the chambers, beneath a ceiling formed of 40 gigantic stone slabs each weighing between 15 and 20 tons, the remnants of a ship were hidden, in a state of excellent preservation. In 1955, the complicated process of securing the more than 400 separate parts of the vessel was begun, which took two years. Exact, small-scale replicas were made of each part. Then came the difficult problem of piecing the model parts together, analogous to the plan followed for the tomb boats of Dahshur, which are approximately 10 meters long and were discovered in 1893. The puzzle pieces fitted together most successfully. At the time of writing, the Cheops ship stands almost completely assembled, in the restoration laboratory below the pyramid. It is 43 meters long, 6 meters broad, and is built over a keelless flat bottom consisting of three cedar boards, ceiled lengthwise and 14 centimeters thick. These boards are fastened together at the edges with treenails made of acacia wood and glued in place, forming a flush surface (ill. 16). In addition, the bottom and side planks are lashed together on the inside of the ship with ropes made of halfa grass. The plank seams were caulked with papyrus bast. Following completion of this extraordinarily well built shell, twelve ribs made of naturally bent wood were inserted and lashed tightly against the bottom boards and side planks, as well as the deck beams.

It seems certain that the ship of Cheops was used as a cult vessel, not as a vehicle for common transport. However, the royal seagoing freighters of the Pharaonic empire were built according to the same principle, in the same construction technique and in at least very similar shape; in such vessels the Egyptian sailors made their voyages to the Levant, Crete, Cyprus and the Lebanon, as well as through the Red Sea to Eritrea and Somalia. In later times the construction of seagoing vessels was further improved, mainly by means of a longitudinal cable running the length of the ship and fastened to the fore and after end. The cable was supported above the deck by fork-ended uprights and its tension could be regulated. Other reinforcements were seizings around the ship ends, and an elastic belting made of cordage along the top strake.

Shiplike vessels play a multifarious role in the religious cults of the Pharaonic empire. They were evidently regarded as the abodes as well as vehicles of the gods. Ceremonial processions with the gods' boats were a regular part of many feast days. The frieze of the temple of Luxor, built under Amenophis III in the 14th century B.C., shows accurate representations of the great ship procession at the aquatic feast of Opet, which was celebrated annually during the second month of the flood of the Nile (ill. 30). In this pageant 50 priests, flanked by high priests adorned in leopard skins, accompanied by drummers and trumpeters, dancing girls and members of the lower clergy scattering holy water and wafting incense burners, carried on their shoulders the boats of the deities Amon, Mut and Chons, as well as that of the Pharaoh, who was venerated as a god-like being, in festive array. A Coptic-Arabic poem of the 14th century indicates that the traditional water feast of Luxor continued to be celebrated long after the Islamization of Egypt.

Though in changed form, the boat procession continues to be part of the customary ceremonial in our time. On the feast day of the patron saint of the mosque, the boat, adorned with multi-colored cloths and a fresh coat of paint, and filled with children who are regarded as bringers of salvation, is paraded solemnly through the town. The people say that the boat belongs to the saint, who wants to go on his sea and river voyages.

The ancient Egyptian creed included the concept of a ferry for the dead: those who had died needed a boat to enter the realm of death. This is how the custom of depositing boat models in graves is explained (ill. 34). Not only in Egypt, but in Mesopotamia and within the Aegean civilizations as well, numerous ship models in wood, earthenware, glass, bronze or silver, dating from the period referred to, have been excavated. The oldest of the ship models to have come to light thus far comes from Mesopotamia; a clay vessel of the Obeid period (about 3200 B.C.), a funerary gift. Such bronze age boat models not only give information on boat shapes and details of construction, but are testimonials to the great age of the cultural use of symbolic ship ornamentation. In the ancient Egyptian civilization eye ornaments in the bow and stern decorations were known, with the preferred motif being plant shapes: the umbels of papyrus, lilies and lotus flowers. The parts serving in the propulsion and steering of the ship were not without their own cultic-symbolic ornamentation. Carved falcons decorated the mast. Sails were made of cloths woven in different colors and embroidered with ornaments. Carved handles of steering oars are known. It seems certain that the choice of colors used in painting a ship, and the design of the ornamention that was incrusted on the upper side planks were also founded on definite customs.

The Pharaohs were the first rulers to elevate navigation, the royal sea trade, to the dignity of a subject for monumental art, causing regular pictorial reports of such voyages to be sculpted in stone or to be painted. As early as 2500 B.C., King Sahure's voyages to the Lebanon were documented in this way. The famous relief of Queen Hatchepsut in the temple of Deir-el-Bahri, approximately 1000 years later, is the most splendid of all ancient artistic representations of ships. It shows the five vessels of the trading expedition to the legendary East African country of Punt, with a detailed, explanatory text, describing the duties of the sailors as well as enumerating the exotic cargo: "The ships were freighted with the produce of the country; quantities of aromatic wood, fresh frankincense, ivory, sacred resin, with dogheaded apes, longtailed monkeys and greyhounds, with leopard skins, and with natives of the country with their children."

In descriptions of ancient Egyptian sea voyages even a sailor myth appears: a report on papyrus, of a shipwreck in the Red Sea. The single survivor was able to reach an island. "Then I heard a sound of thunder and thought it was a wave. Trees broke and the earth quaked. I uncovered my face and found that a serpent had drawn near. It was 45 feet long and its beard was 2 feet long. Its body was covered with gold and its eyebrows were real lapis lazuli." Fortunately the monster was goodnatured, received the sailor with kindness, prophesied his rescue by a Pharaonic ship and made him a present of frankincense at leavetaking. The oldest pictorial document of a legendary report of this nature comes from Crete: an engraved signet shows a shipman fighting with a sea monster, whose open maw is raised threateningly above the ship's bulwark (ill. p. 49).

Phoenician Sea Voyages

The period of approximately 1800 to 1400 B.C. was the golden age of the Cretan-Minoan sea trade and seapower, the so-called "Thalassocracy". However, there is no exact information as regards the shape and build of the Aegean vessels. From the 12th to the 8th century the Phoenicians were the supreme seafarers of the Mediterranean. The Greeks gave them their name, which signifies "trader in purple". They referred to themselves as Sidonians and their name for their coastal homeland was Canaan. At Sidon, Tyros, Akkon and Byblos they built ship upon ship; they undertook the most daring long-distance voyages, began the systematic founding of colonial establishments; and yet they have left behind neither illustrations nor written accounts that might give us information about their vessels. At last, a new wreck find began to shed some light in the darkness.

In 1959 the archeologist Peter Throckmorton, with the help of Turkish fishermen, discovered fragments of an ancient sunken ship near the western shore of the Gulf of Adalia in Anatolia. The spot was near the Cape of Gelidonia at a depth of 27 meters. A team of the University of Pennsylvania, assisted by the French navy diver Frédéric Dumas, in June 1960 began the careful salvaging of the remnants of the ship. Archeologists descended to the sea bottom with light diving equipment and photographed and charted the area in a grid of decimeter squares. Following this, photographs of the visible portions of the wreck and the remnants of the cargo were made. The final stage of the operation consisted of a thorough search of the bottom sand by means of suction pumps. A clear picture of the situation of the wreck was thus produced. What twenty years earlier no scientist would have dared to believe, had become a fact: here was a find of a bronze age ship, which it was possible to date through the radiocarbon method as belonging to the period around 1250 B.C. The successful excavator, George Bass, became famous as the explorer of the oldest wreck so far known.

The Gelidonia vessel was a plank boat built of oak and cypress, about 10 meters long, having a cargo capacity of roughly 1 to 2 tons. It was laden, obviously at Cyprus, with bar copper, each bar weighing somewhat more than 20 kilograms, carefully stowed in mats. In addition, it carried baskets filled with bronze scrap and lead, also some tin in bars, as well as a jar containing painted glass beads. Other items salvaged from the wreck were anvils, hammers, chisels, hole-punches, rasps and one whetstone. The crew quarters were aft and yielded up the ship's lamp and some containers for provisions made of leather and pottery. The skipper had had three complete sets of weights for balances and a cylindrical seal found aft was surely his property. The fibers of which the mats were made, and the shape of the lamp and seal, proved that this must have been a ship of the Lebanon, a small Phoenician ore carrier.

One common characteristic of shipbuilding techniques of ancient Mediterranean times is the method of flush-sided (carvel) fastening of the hull planks by means of inserted treenails. It is the hallmark of Mediterranean origin, just as the lapstrake (clinker) construction is the characteristic feature of vessels of the northern European coasts and of some maritime regions of India and China. Both techniques have their roots in the common principle of shell construction. As far as outer shape is concerned, the Egyptian vessels may have borne a more or less close resemblance to papyrus rafts. It seems certain that the Aegean boats showed different contours, influenced by sharply rising boat ends. It is possible that they evolved from log canoes by way of the intermediate stage of the bottom shell type, in which case we would find that in the Levant, during the bronze age or perhaps earlier, a similar evolution of the log boat to the keel boat took place to that which is archeologically demonstrable for a later period in Scandinavia.

It was not long before the Phoenician ships extended their range outside the Mediterranean to the Spanish Atlantic coast. Near Tunis, on Malta, Sicily, Sardinia and near Cadiz, they founded "filial" or staple ports, establishments under military guard administered by Tyros and Sidon. In southern Spain, Tartessos was a renowned staple port for the sea trade with Britannic tin and Irish copper, as well as the "new town" of Carthage, founded around 800 B.C. Legends, documentary reports of this era, and later, Greco-Roman commentaries unfold the vast range of the sea rovings of these ancient Lebanese. In alliance with King Solomon of Israel, they advanced about 950 B.C. from the Red Sea southward as far as India and Southeast Africa. Commissioned by an Egyptian ruler, Phoenician ships untertook, about 600 B.C., the incredibly venturesome circumnavigation of Africa from the east, southward and then westward, which for the following two thousand years was to become an impossibility.

Taking their departure from Carthage in 525 B.C., they succeeded in carrying out a well-organized reconnaissance along the coast of West Africa, reaching the Cameroon Mountain. Other Phoenicians got as far as the "tin islands"—Britain—and the Azores, where their coins have been found. Not long ago the debate regarding the authenticity of an ancient Sidonian inscription found on the Brazilian coast in 1874 aroused the question of the possibility of Phoenician ships having reached South America, which brings this additional trade route within the realm of possibilities. Generally speaking, scholars of the history of civilization nowadays tend to consider the factual content of the ancient seafaring legends and sailor myths to be less remote from truth than formerly, and probably rightly so.

31 Relief of a (Phoenician?) diere from the palace of the Assyrian king Sennacherib at Nineveh, about 690 B.C. (after Björn Landström).

Greeks and Romans

The long voyages of the Phoenicians are the high point of Mediterranean navigation. Beginning with this period, the prevalent types of ships in the maritime affairs of the Etruscans, Greeks and Romans were of two kinds. Of these, the rowing vessel having more than one tier of oars is presumed to be a Phoenician invention. The oldest pictures of such ships date around 700 B.C. In boats of this class the rowing crew was seated on different levels; the upper tier of sweeps was supported on the gunwale; in the lower one the sweeps projected through holes in the sides of the ship. In later times the Greeks introduced a perfection of this idea in equipping their large triremes with yet another, third rank of oarsmen, manning sweeps pivoted on outriggers projecting from the sides.

32 Sgraffito from the wall of a merchant's house at Pompei near Naples. The ship "Europa" represents the standard type of Roman cargo vessel, showing the characteristic rig of the period, consisting of mainsail and foresail (after Amadeo Maiuri).

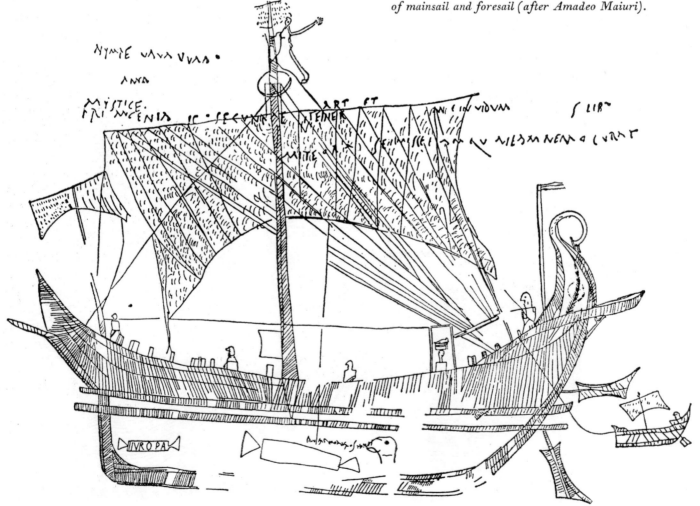

33 The 12 meter raft "Ra 2" under the command of the Norwegian anthropologist Thor Heyerdahl, with a crew of eight men, crossed the Atlantic from Morocco to the West Indies, sailing through the Northeast Trades. The voyage was begun in May 1970, arrival was in July the same year. The raft was made by South American Aymara Indians from bundles of papyrus from the Nile.

34 *Ancient Egyptian boat model used as a funerary gift in the period of the Middle Empire, approximately 2000–1700 B. C.*

35 *So-called "Norican Sky-Boat Rider", clay model barely 20 centimeters long; found in 1948 on a Celtic ritual site on the Magdalensberg near Klagenfurt in Carinthia (Austria), to be dated about 660 B. C. The expressive miniature sculpture may have had some connection with the complex of myths of the Deluge, which are as old as the origins of early primeval societies.*

36 *Ancient Egyptian relief of oarsmen, from the Temple of Deir-el-Bahri, around 1500* B. C.

37 *Relief on the tomb of the shipbuilder Longidienus of Ravenna, 3rd century A.D. The master is shown in the act of shaping a frame or rib. Lionel Casson in 1963 identified this representation as proof of the ancients' practicing the technology of shell-boat construction.*

38 *Boatbuilder Johan Matsson of Saitarova, Norrland, Sweden, fashioning a wooden frame. Master Matsson performed in the year 1958 the same work, using the same kind of tool, in the same position as his colleague 1700 years earlier in the time of the Roman antique.*

"And he set to cutting timber, and his work went busily. Twenty trees in all he felled, and then trimmed them with the axe of bronze, and deftly smoothed them, and over them made straight the line. Meanwhile Calypso, the fair goddess, brought him augers, so he bored each piece and jointed them together, and then made all fast with treenails and dowels. Wide as is the floor of a broad ship of burden, which some man well skilled in carpentry may trace him out, of such beam did Odysseus fashion his broad raft. And thereat he wrought, and set up the deckings, fitting them to the close-set uprights, and finished them off with long gunwales, and therein he set a mast, and a yardarm fitted thereto, and moreover he made him a rudder to guide the craft. And he fenced it with wattled osier withies from stem to stern, to be a bulwark against the wave, and piled up wood to back them. Meanwhile Calypso, the fair goddess, brought him web of cloth to make his sails; and these too he fashioned very skilfully. And he made fast therein braces and halyards and sheets, and at last he pushed the raft with levers down to the fair salt sea."

The Odyssey of Homer, Book V
(translated into English prose by S. H. Butcher and A. Lang)
The Modern Library, New York

Freighters in Roman times, particularly the wheat carriers of the Egypt-Italy route, were of respectable dimensions and had a cargo capacity of up to 1000 tons. The old scholarly opinion, to the effect that the single-masted square rig was the only one known and used, has been invalidated by recent research. In quite recent times, in an Etruscan tomb ascribed to approximately 450 B.C., a colored mural painting of a two-masted square-rigger was discovered by Italian archeologists.

Lastly, let us consider the subject of symbolical decorations of ships' sterns in classical Greece. An entire complex of "sacred" symbols was concentrated in the after parts of ships, made up of the figuratively carved ornamentation of the sternpost, the *aphlaston;* the statue of a deity *(tutela)* and of a ceremonial cruciform standard *(stylis)*, and of strips of purple woolen cloth *(taenia)* set flying like flags, which testified to the execution of sacrificial acts which, it was hoped, would be of beneficial effect. When entering or leaving port, the stern of a ship was also decorated with laurel wreaths. The oldest known symbol, belonging to Homer's time (8th century B.C.), is the stern configuration, originally a system of geometrical lines or a fishtail motif, possibly expressive of obsolete magical concepts. Statues of deities, cultic standards and sacrificial ribbons, on the other hand, occur only from the beginning of the 4th century B.C. on, and seem to reflect a less ancient cult comprising sacrifices and prayers. It appears probable that the total sacral complex, composed of diverse elements, which caused the stern of the ship to be regarded as the "sacred place", indicates a situation in which the older beliefs of fishermen and sailors were overlaid by attributes belonging to the later state religion.

We should not omit to mention modern ship research in the Mediterranean, which has presented us with results which no one would have dared dream about fifty years ago. In 1934, at Cannes on the French Riviera, the first Mediterranean sport divers club for the furtherance of skin diving, without helmet, pressurized diving suit and signal rope, was founded. Beginning with the year 1938 the Viennese biologist Hans Hass tested this method in the Adriatic Sea. In 1943, Yves Cousteau made his first diving experiments with an adjustable pressure-breathing apparatus. During the years following, a spirit of friendly collaboration developed between the submarine research group of the French Navy, headed by Yves Cousteau and Frédéric Dumas, and the archeologists of the National Monuments Service of the coastal area around the Rhone delta and the Riviera. An antique wrecked ship having been located not far from Marseilles, in the vicinity of the island of Grand Congloué, in a depth of 30 to 40 meters, the provincial conservator decided at last in 1952, to risk a first "submarine excavation" with the aid of the diving group. Although the result did not come up to the great expectations attached to the venture, Grand Congloué nevertheless became the point of departure for a special branch of research: submarine archeology. The early methods were rapidly improved. Today we have, as a first palpable result of international collaboration, a large-scale cartographic inventory of wrecked ships from the Etruscan to the Byzantine periods, that are within reach. It is now known that the bottom of entire areas of the Mediterranean Sea, for instance the narrows between Corsica and Sardinia, or the sea of the Cyclades, is as it were paved with amphoras, the cargo containers of ancient wrecks.

The ultimate aim of which Yves Cousteau dreamed, to present the world with a Greek or Roman ship salvaged from the depths of the ocean, will probably never be accomplished by submarine archeology. The roughness of the sea bed, fierce currents, but above all the centuries-long activity of the voracious shipworms, remove such a haul from the realm of possibilities. We will have to wait until we get a second chance, in the course of some harbor dredging or airfield construction, river regulation or draining operation. For a first chance had already come once: in 1930 at Lake Nemi.

This small piece of water is situated a scant 20 kilometers southeast of Rome in the Albanese hills. The population thereabouts knew of stories of sunken vessels of "primordial" times. In 1895 divers were able to prove the truth of the legend. Two big wrecks were discovered in depths of 5 and 22 meters. In 1928 the salvage operations were begun. Technically speaking this was a grandiose enterprise, in the course of which the level of the lake was lowered by 25 meters by means of a subterranean canal. The first wreck emerged in 1929, the other one the year following. Coin finds dated the vessels around the year 170. They were gigantic ships, more than 70 meters long. Nobody had an explanation of the purpose they once may have served. It hardly matters whether their creation was the result of Imperial whim or whether they were built for some cultic ceremonial; it is certain that both Nemi ships were built exactly like normal freighters. For the first time in history, unequivocal information regarding all the many construction details became available. "Caligula's ships"—Caligula being the ruler of Rome at the time of their origin—demonstrated the principle of Mediterranean shell construction. Bottom and side planks were dowelled together, the ribs closely spaced at intervals barely the width of one of the timbers. Planks and inserted ribs were fastened together with bronze nails.

The destiny of the Nemi ships was evidently ruled by Nemesis, the goddess of revenge. In 1939 both vessels were at last housed beneath the roof of a specially erected museum, after a difficult move on sledges. Close study of these unique objects was about to commence when war prevented it. During the battle of Rome, on the last day of May 1944, there was an air attack on a German anti-aircraft battery positioned in the museum area. The bombs hit the target and in a few hours the Nemi ships were a heap of cinders.

39 Reconstruction of the stowage of amphoras in the wreck of Albenga, Liguria, salvaged in 1961 and exhibited in the Museo Navale Romano at Albenga.
The Roman sailors distinguished between bulk and general cargoes. For the transport of wine, olive oil, fish, snails, fruit and leguminous vegetables standardized ceramic containers of the kind illustrated were used. The wreck of Grand Congloué in southern France contained about 3000 amphoras, each of a capacity of between 20 to 25 kilograms. Their shape and stopper seals permitted a reconstruction of the last voyage of this ship: departing from Delos in the Aegean Sea, it touched at the South Italian Campania on its way to the port of destination, Massilia, the Marseilles of today.

At the end of the twenties, the excavations of the magnificent city cultures of Mohenjo-Daro and Harappa in the valley of the Indus, of An-yang on the Hoang-Ho, and the discovery of the bronze culture of Dongson in Vietnam, aroused wide and merited public attention. Indefatigable spadework since those beginnings has produced something like the crude outlines of these early class civilizations. Almost each new dig brings fresh surprises to the surface.

What kind of vessels were the ships of the ancient civilizations between the Persian Gulf and the Yellow Sea?

In Mesopotamia, the Sumerians and Akkadians, in their cuneiform texts whose beginnings are placed around the year 3000 B.C., have left copious material for the study of the city populations along the Euphrates and Tigris. Among others, shipyard documents were found, from which we may see that the Mesopotamian ships of the 3rd millennium were plank boats built according to the shell method. The plank strakes of fir were fastened with treenails made of laurel wood. The ship was coated with asphalt on the outside and seasoned with fish oil inside. The fitted transverse braces were hewn out of naturally bent mulberry tree timbers. Sumerians and Akkadians imported their boatbuilding woods from overseas, a center for reshipment being the Bahrein Islands. Numerous reliefs and pictures on seals (ill. 40), as well as boat models made of bitumen, clay and silver, show vessels which incontrovertibly argue an innovative change in ship construction and a departure from the tradition of rush fagot rafts. Old Mesopotamian texts yield some indications concerning the course this important technological evolution may have taken. The oldest Sumerian ideographs for "ship" are sign-like representations of flat and tied vehicles with bent-up ends. This symbol evidently signifies rafts made of rush fagots. It can also stand for "water craft" as well as for "boat of the gods", "crescent of the moon", "fishing boat", but likewise "ship going to sea". Newer texts mention wooden vessels and refer to planks, dowels and braces. Besides this, the Akkadian documents also speak of water vehicles used by the people, i.e. the frame type *quppu*, furthermore a raft made of inflated animal skins called *kalakku*. The terms *guffa* and *kellek*, in keeping with the traditional form and construction of these vessels, have remained unchanged for nearly 5000 years in the Country of the Two Rivers.

40 Ship picture—probably of a raft made of bundles of rushes—projection of an unrolled Old-Mesopotamian seal from Uruk, Period IV, about 2900 B.C

"At the bright quay he stepped into the sail ship,
And a wind blew, and his ship glided forth.
With the oar, he guided his ship on the broad sea..."

This Akkadian poem is proof, as much and as surely as the shipyard reports and the boat models placed in tombs, of the fact that in the Mesopotamia of the 3rd millennium B.C. sailing was already known. The rig consisted of a square sail spread from a yard suspended transversely across the ship.

The inscriptions at Ur, Eridu, Uruk and Babylon testify to the use of names for ships in these early times; many poetical names have been preserved for posterity: Roaring Gale, Bright Wild Cow, Stream of Life, Ibex of the Ocean, Lord of the Stream, Ship of Supreme Delight.

41 Scratch-incised ship picture on a shard of an urn in polychromic ceramic of the Indus civilization of Mohenjo-Daro, 3rd millennium B C. (after E. J. H. Mackey).

Few pictorial representations of ships have come to our knowledge so far from the urban culture in the valley of the Indus and on the coast of the Gujerat, which came into being around 2500 B.C. These show various types which we interpret as rush fagot rafts (or else boats in raft shape), and as plank boats with tripod mast, square sail with yard, and steering oar shipped alongside (ill. 41). The fact that seals from the Indus have been found on the Bahrein Islands and in Mesopotamia has suggested the early existence of sea trade between the Indus and the Euphrates-Tigris delta. A proof of this was furnished by the most recent excavations of the seaport city of Lothal on the Gujerat coast, which forms part of the Indus culture and where a masonry dock of very impressive dimensions was found: it is more than 2000 meters long and 350 meters wide; the quay walls, made of brick, are 4 meters high.

We cannot know, of course, whether the illustrations found in the Indus region represent domestic or foreign vessels, but present ethnology offers a hint towards clarification of the problem. On the Indus, the vessels of the working population are made to this day in the shell type of construction, but with dowelled planks, which is an isolated technique in this area. On the Gujerat coast to a point north of Bombay, the side planks of the boats are fastened together with countersunk spikes (ill. 16). Technically speaking, nail-spiking is very close to dowelling, and perhaps represents a variant of the method. The fact of these two building methods existing in an area otherwise using the technique of lacing the planks together clearly indicates relics of a past period. When such traditions are examined, it seems hard to disprove that India too must have had a period of innovation in shipbuilding during its bronze age, a transition to plank construction with treenail fastening.

China

Up to now, well-founded information relative to Chinese prehistoric water craft is lacking. We do not doubt that they had existed among the fishermen of the late stone age of the Yellow River and the coast of Shantung: certainly there were rafts of the rush fagot or inflated animal skin types, and perhaps also log canoes and timber rafts, for northern China formerly had more forests than now. The question of how the highly developed bronze metallurgy of the early cities in the valley of the Hoang-Ho had been able to do without navigation for the transportation of crude ore, cannot be answered with assurance by any of the relevant scientific disciplines. No artistic or literary references to ships of the time before the 5th century B.C. have come to light: neither seals nor reliefs, no scratch incisions in clay, no vase decor nor boat models; even detailed texts are lacking. Confronted with this paucity of material, the findings of ethnographical research remain the only reliable source for clarification of the problem.

According to oral tradition current among the Chinese boatmen, the boats of the Hoang-Ho area are regarded as more old-fashioned than those of the Yangtze River. On the upper reaches of the Yellow River (Hoang-Ho) there were, in earlier times, bottom plank boats built on the shell principle, with planks of fir wood and fastened with bent nail staples. On the Manchurian rivers inserted treenails were used, and described by Dutch chroniclers as early as 1671 as a common technique worthy of special mention, of Chinese ways of fastening boat plank strakes. These unequivocal characteristics of the oldest Chinese shipbuilding ways in the North—shell construction and plank dowelling—suggest the thought that there may have occurred a "leap" in prehistoric development of the civilization in the Hoang-Ho region, due to which the plank type could be created without replacing the various predecessors. To such a hypothesis, the core of truth concealed in the ancient Chinese myths relating to the "invention" of planked vessels and of net-fishing by god-like heroes or legendary rulers would be a corroborating counterpart. However, the question of what was the predecessor—log canoe, rush-fagot raft or timber raft—must remain open for the time being. The fact that very diverse elements were fused together in early periods to form what has become Chinese civilization, makes it almost probable that still other shipbuilding traditions influenced, for example, the construction of junks which in some regions are built in a curious variation of lapstrake or clinker planking. It is not impossible that in Chinese aquatic areas having vessels deriving from an ancient tradition of frame construction, frame building with an outer plank skin may have developed in early historic times.

The old wherries of the Hoang-Ho carried a simple square sail with yard, and were steered by means of an oar shipped across the transom and parallel to the longitudinal axis of the vessel. This corresponds to the vessels represented in the mural paintings of the Buddhist cave monastery of Tun Huang, which date from the 10th century (ill. 45).

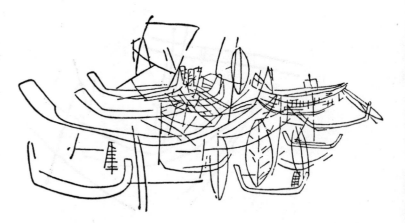

42 Representation of boats on a wall drawing in the large stone tomb of Midorikawa, Japan, 5th century B.C. Some vessels are obviously sailing boats (after Edward Kidder).

On the River

In the evening falls the first hoar rime
frost seizes my little boat.
On the shore, maple trees are still glowing,
but full of melancholy
is autumn in the strange land.

The barren billows of the River
are lost to sight in broad bays of water,
the Sun is sinking below the horizon.
Beneath wooded heights I halt my boat,
and I hear the screams of monkeys.

The Milky Way at midnight
changes direction; I leave my quiet berth
and gaze into the flooding darkness.
The night wind is whimpering and weeping,
monotonously rustle the waves.

Sandbanks are gleaming beyond,
and slowly the great Moon
emerges from the black water.
Her beams cause me to think
yearningly of my friends far away.

Li Tai-bo, 701–762

At Anchor

Little sleep and much discomfort—the traveller
rises at midnight and gazes in the direction of home.
Brightly the sand shines in the moonlight flooding the shores.
The sails are white with the dew that causes the ship to gleam.
As we approach the Sea, the River grows wide and wider,
As we progress into Autumn, the nights grow long and longer.
Thirty times we have slept already on the fog-veiled billows,
but still we have not yet made our Port of Hangchou.

Po Chü-i, 772–846

Southeast Asia

In the Gulf of Tonkin, situated between the delta of the Sikiang in Kwangtung and the delta of the Red River in North Vietnam, we encounter the bronze age civilization of Dongson, which began in the course of the 1st millennium B.C. and which was discovered in 1924. In subsequent periods the manufacturing of bronze objects spread over the entire coastal region including Malaya, the Moluccas and the Philippines, carried by a genuine maritime civilization. In contrast to the Hoang-Ho culture of the Chinese North, the Dongson culture has left behind many representations of ships, mostly as decoration of the characteristic ceremonial kettle drums. Crescent-shaped outlines of boats with ornamented sides and beautiful stem decorations, clearly showing a helmsman with steering oar shipped over the side and the crew of paddlers, embellish the bronze drum bodies (ill. 43). Instruments of this kind continue to be used in the area of the old Dongson culture up to the present. In the same region some old-fashioned boatbuilding methods have survived in our time, e.g. plank dowelling. Another relic of ancient times is found in other places, where during the process of hewing out the side planks, projecting "clamps" are left standing, which serve, after completion of the bottom shell, for the fastening of the inserted ribs.

From the foregoing we may state that four common characteristics are found in ancient water craft of the early bronze age civilizations in the Near and Far East. Plank boats were built by the shell method. Their carvel-laid side planks were fastened one to another either with treenails (dowels) or with double-ended spikes; inserted bracing ribs were occasionally lashed to projecting clamps. The rig was a transverse square rig with yard. We assume that these characteristics are signs of some common prehistoric origin of innovative ship construction. The significance of boatbuilding technology and plank fastening methods as guideposts for worldwide comparative ship research has hitherto been ignored. In advance of others, Edmond Paris and Robert Heine-Geldern have marked a basic line of approach to this kind of research.

Remnants of shell construction with dowelled or spiked fastening of side planks have lasted into our times: on the Black and Caspian Seas, at the Indus and Ganges, on the coast of the Gujerat; on the Hoang-Ho, in Manchuria, Yunnan, Japan and on the shores bordering the Gulf of Thailand, in Vietnam, Cambodia and Malacca; on Taiwan, the Philippines, on Borneo, the Sunda Islands and the Moluccas. The lashing of ribs to projections protruding from the side planks appears as a special variant on the island of Botel Tobago off Taiwan and on the Moluccas, as well as on the Melanesian Solomon Islands; finally on Fiji, Samoa and Tonga. Herein the Melanesian and West Polynesian plank boats again present a regional shading: they are built in the shell mode and have fitted ribs or bulkheads, but in conjunction with sewn, not dowelled, side planks.

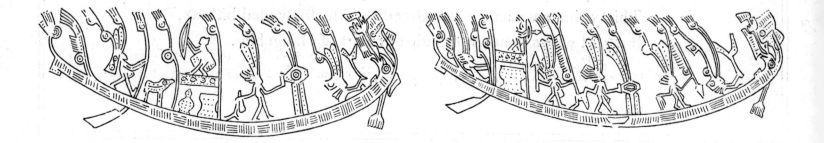

Left 43: Ritual ship picture in the ornamental border of a bronze kettledrum of the Dongson culture of Ngoc Lu, Vietnam. From: Franz Heger, Alte Metalltrommeln aus Südostasien, Leipzig 1902.

44 Seagoing ship with three-masted lug rig. Detail from a mural painting in cave No. 2 of the Indian Buddhist Monastery of Ajanta, about 5th century.

45 Boat with square sail. Detail from a wall painting in cave No. 288
of the Buddhist cloister Tun Huang in Northwest China, about 900.

46 *A view of junks in Hongkong harbor, seen from underneath the roof of a market boat (Sampan).*

Anywhere in the world, navigation under adverse conditions is liable to become a dangerous battle with elemental forces, the outcome of which does not depend exclusively on the human will. The protection of the all-important vessel, from which depends the safety of the crew, is of main concern in the thinking and feeling of ship people. We in the West have attempted, in the last two or three hundred years, to solve these problems by having recourse to science, i.e. in a purely rational manner. During the millennia preceding our era, maritime traditions were permeated by ancient religious folk creeds of various origins. In the comprehension of fishermen and seafarers of the primeval social organizations, whose understanding of natural laws was undeveloped, cultic ceremonial operated on the level of an illusionary consciousness, as faith, with the aid of which they hoped to propitiate and influence natural and social forces not controllable by other means.

Seamen have always shown a marked preference for folk-religious magic. Concepts of magic and sorcery arise where human consciousness, confronted with the elemental forces of Nature feels unsure of its intellectual and physical resources. Magic was practiced with an infinity of charms, ritual acts and symbols. Perhaps not every orna-

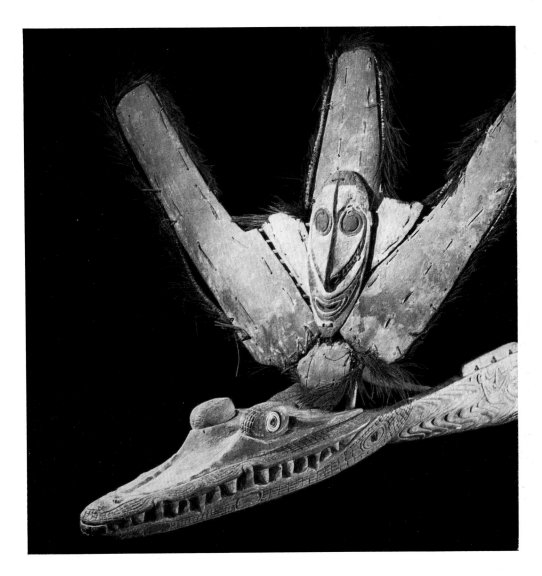

47/48 *Boat prows from New Guinea,*
decorated with traditional crocodile heads.

ment, but certainly a great proportion of those found in ships, must have had apotropaic virtue in the eyes of primitive society, or else had its origin in a traditional sign connected with defensive magic against natural forces. Since earliest times certain parts of the ship have borne luck-bringing or protective insignia; principally the fore and after ends of the hull. The motifs were either taken from nature or were artistic statements in the form of paintings or sculpture. Carved animal shapes were frequently used for stem decoration, for instance horned bulls' or rams' heads, heads of horses and dragons, also goosenecks and fishtails. Crocodiles, sea birds, dolphins and serpents

also served as models. Often such figures were themselves decorated, inlaid with shells and hung with strings of beads, leafy garlands and wreaths. In the early periods some of the animal motifs used as stem decorations may have had a connection with totemistic concepts. Whether remnants of totemism or symbols of counter-magic, the custom of decorating the stems of vessels is an expression of a very ancient folk practice handed down by tradition through immense spans of time.

49 *Junk in the harbor of Hongkong.*
Plank boats built non-industrially continue to exist in greater numbers
than is commonly thought. The number of junks on the Yangtze river
alone was estimated to be anywhere between 30 and 50 thousand a few
years ago. In Indonesia more than 175,000 non-motorized fishing
craft were registered recently.

50 *Boat dwelling of the Sampan type in one of the "floating suburbs" near Hongkong, which are inhabited and autonomously administered by special groups of the fishing population. These Tanka and Hoklo people were distinguishable from their shore-dwelling neighbors by their dialect, customs and mode of living. For centuries they were legally defamed as "maritime pariahs" and excluded from public schooling, exercising a craft or engaging in trade.*

51 The Gayasa, the splendid, big flat-bottomed boat of the lower Nile, carries an impressively tall lateen rig.

Up to this point we have not discussed any material relating to archeological wreck finds either from America or Africa. Representations of ships abound in the art of Mexico, of the Mayas and Incas. There are mural paintings in temples, drawings in Indian pictographic documents, sculptures, jewelry and ceramic raft models (ill. 58). But such works of art do not yield up all the details of construction of the vessels they portray. Here again we are confined to draw conclusions from the ethnographical observations made during the period between the 16th and the 19th centuries.

During the so-called "classical" and "post-classical" phases of American civilizations, numerous prototypes belonging to all three classes of shipbuilding technologies were in use for water transport. In the colligative group there are rafts made of logs, of fagots of rushes, and of inflated animal skins; in the frame technique, we find serviceable skin boats. Technical progress beyond the original state of the prototype is recognizable in the manufacturing of treebark vessels by the Indians of North America. In central California the Chumash had sewn plank boats, while in the extreme south of Chile the Alakaluf and Yamana used multiple-unit, sewn bark slab boats. In the Caribbean Sea, as Columbus noted with astonishment in 1502, extremely able, sewn bottom shell boats developed from dugouts and of great cargo capacity—the *piraguas*—were cruising everywhere; this type was also used by the Mayas for their commercial voyages.

52 Rafts of Lake Margherita in southern Ethiopia. These are vessels between 7 and 10 meters long, made of 12 trunks of the ambatch cork tree, fastened together with treenails made of acacia wood. Propulsion is by poling and they are used by tribesmen belonging to the hunting caste of the east Kushitic lake island tribes of the Giditjo and Gatami, for fishing and water hunting, whereas the *Galla inhabiting the areas bordering these lakes neither make water vehicles nor eat fish or hippo meat. The hunting and fishing castes are held to be "unclean" and legally inferior, and do not own land or raise cattle. The women of the fisher folk make pottery and do weaving (after Eike Haberland).*

Similar bottom shell boats were used by the Indians of the northwest coast of America, mainly in the Canadian territory of today.

Sails, although of unidentified type, were already in use before the arrival of the first Europeans, in the Caribbean Sea as well as on the Andean coast of Ecuador and Peru, as is learned from Indian tradition and from the vocabulary of the respective language groups. A thinkable prototype might have resembled the rectangular rush-mat sail of the sedge rafts of the Uro of Lake Titicaca (ill. 5), which is rigged with a tripod mast. The trading rafts of the Inca Empire, of imposing dimensions (ill. 77), whose extensive sea voyages along the west coast are well documented and the seaworthiness of which Thor Heyerdahl has proven by way of his voyage in 1947 in "Kon-Tiki"— 4300 nautical miles from Peru to the East Polynesian Tuamotu Islands—probably sailed under some kind of triangular fore-and-aft sails in the early times, later under some form of square rig. With their ingenious daggerboard technique of steering, they were even able to go to windward.

Our not overly abundant knowledge of ancient American water craft may be called almost lavish compared to the meager information relative to navigation in the western and central Sudanese feudal civilizations of Niger and Lake Chad, the ancient kingdoms of Ghana, Mali and Kanem, and the states of the Bantu people. Moorish geographers tell of Malinese voyages across the Atlantic around the year 1300. We are unable to form an opinion of what kind of vessel may have been employed. Possibly they were large log canoes, of the kind used by the Bidjugo (ill. p. 8), the Kru and the Duala. During the 19th century in the river regions of Niger, Benue, Shari and Chad, and in the area of the great Uganda lakes there were unconnected zones of distribution of sewn plank boats, the only ones of the kind in "black" Africa. In particular, the origin of the Uganda boats has already caused lively controversy. James Hornell stipulated a Malayan-Arabian influence coming from the Kenya coast. Others envisaged ancient contact with the Nubian Nile region, perhaps to the kingdom of Meroë. A third argued for local development by the Bantu people in the lake region. Let us hope that research to come will eventually be able to close this gap in our information.

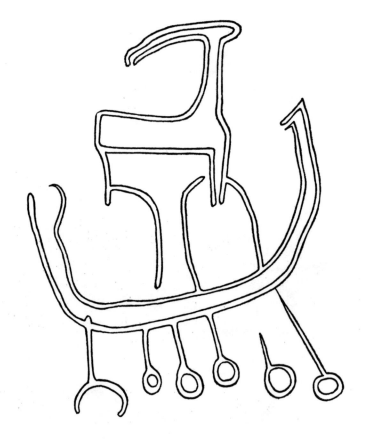

53a) Rock picture from Nubia (after Reinhold Engelmayer).

Questions of Dating

Up to now there are no signs of water craft of the old stone age in the maritime region between the Bay of Biscay and the Gulf of Finland. For the middle stone age the picture is different. Around 8000 B.C. the gradual transition from the ice age to present-day geographical, climatic and ecological conditions began in northern Europe. Vast, dense evergreen forests covered the land from Scotland to the Urals and into Siberia, interspersed with birch groves; later elms, linden, alder, poplar and oak became domesticated. Around 6500 B.C. the mouths of the Meuse and Rhine were in the vicinity of the Humber, while the Elbe emptied into the North Sea north of Heligoland. The Baltic extended into the Arkona Basin between Rügen and Skane. The countless landlocked waters abounded in fish, their shores were frequented by game of all sorts and provided nesting areas for the bird population. Berries, mushrooms, herbs and nuts, fish, fowl and game, aquatic mammals and clams offered bountiful food for a rapidly increasing, specialized population of fishermen and beach gatherers. The civilization of these groups began to form as early as the period between 8000 and 7000 B.C. At a somewhat later date we find them established from England to Karelia; from one of the first major finds in Denmark, they have received the collective name of the Maglemose civilization. Other groups of "littoral gatherers" existed in Portugal, on the coast of the Basques, and in Brittany. For their food-gathering purposes the Maglemose people developed equipment of such effectiveness that much of it has continued to remain in use through these thousands of years: e.g. barbed fishhooks, fish grains and basket fish traps, nets with their complex knots and with stone weights and floats made of pine or rushes.

To this coastal civilization of the middle stone age belong the earliest examples of water craft of which we have knowledge. These are the paddle finds of Star Carr near the mouth of the Humber in England, of Duvensee near Lübeck, and of Holmegaard in Zealand. The paddle of Star Carr and the entire settlement, which was only a seasonal one, is dated at around 7500 B.C. Also assigned to the middle stone age are the two finds of dugouts at Perth in Scotland, and at Pesse in northern Holland (around 6300 B.C.). Both boats are made of pine logs. No log canoes were found, however, in connection with paddle finds belonging to the oldest fishing camps of the Maglemose people. It remains uncertain whether they had light, skin or bark-covered vessels made in the frame technique. During the 19th century (and before), this technology was indigenous in northern Europe, in Ireland and Wales, as well as in Lapland, northern Siberia, Canada and Greenland. The present state of our information does not permit an answer to the question whether, in the middle stone age in northern Europe, both types of technology were simultaneously in use with the same groups of coastal gatherers, or whether some groups practiced only the shell method of making log boats, while others confined themselves to the building of hide-covered frame boats.

The pattern of finds remains unchanged during the centuries of the late stone age. Some few log canoes are known, chiefly from Denmark, England and Scotland; but also from the region of the Alps and lower Alps. No trace of plank boats belonging to this period has come to light; they are demonstrable only for the late bronze age.

53 b) Rock picture from Norway (after Sverre Marstrander).

The Problem of Prototypes

The oldest northern European plank boat came to our knowledge in the English find at North Ferriby, not far from the mouth of the Humber. At this site the remains of three vessels, assigned to the period 850–600 B.C., were collected between 1947 and 1963. The boat find of Hjortspring on the Danish-Slesvig island of Als is tentatively dated around 300 B.C., while the boat from Halsnøy in central Norway is a little more recent still. Then there is the fragment of a wreck from Valderøy, also in central Norway, which is doubtless very ancient but cannot be dated with any degree of certainty. The most recent find in this line is the oldest ship found in the North Sea and Baltic area, the famous vessel at Nydam in Schleswig, discovered in 1863, which belongs in the 4th century A.D. Approximately of the same period is the boat found by Björke-Hille on the coast of Central Sweden in Gästrikland.

A summary of these six finds from the period between 700 B.C. and A.D. 300 shows that the lengths of the boats varied between 5 and 23 meters. Their functions, too, are likely to have been very diverse; probably as ferry boats,

53 Ritual representations of ships in rock pictures. Scandinavian rock pictures were already known in the 19th century. More recently they have been methodically surveyed and published. Shiplike vessels are dominant among the pictorial motifs. Soviet archeologists published in 1936 and 1970 a documentation of the rock engravings of Carelia and of the White Sea coast, with abundant illustrations of ships. Frobenius and Schweinfurth were the first to take inventories of rock pictures in Africa. The result of more recent Austrian researches was presented in 1965 by Engelmayer in a volume of plates specially dedicated to rock pictures of ships in Nubia. Here, water craft occupy a second place in frequency, animal representations being first. Röder's work, published in 1959, has acquainted us with the ship pictures of the rock paintings of New Guinea. Only one factor can be seen with assurance as being common to all these images of ships in rock murals and carvings, spread over so vast an area: the enormous symbolical importance that water craft—no matter of what kind or construction—must have had in the religious concepts of primeval social groups of certain particular regions, being regarded as "ships of deities" and valued accordingly. Ritual or sacred places were decorated with pictures of such vessels.

53 c) Rock picture from the White Sea (after W. J. Ravdonikas).

53 d) Rock picture from Western New Guinea (after Josef Röder).

Evolution of Frame Construction with Planks

fishing vessels and boats for long voyages. One is almost reluctant to draw conclusions from such disparate material. However, the results of typological comparison yield a remarkably unified picture and testify clearly to a certain tendency of evolution. All six finds are plank boats of the shell construction type. Apparently in the early times softwood was the preferred material, i.e. pine and linden wood. Exceptions did occur, the Ferriby find being of oak, as was also the case with one of the two Nydam boats. All six have pointed ends when seen in the plan view, with stem and sternpost. All show as a main characteristic of their construction a stout bottom plank; the Halsnøy and Nydam boats have a first suggestion of a shallow vertical keel. Stem and bottom planks show marks of hollowing. The specimens with several side planks belong to two formal groups: Ferriby has flush-sided carvel plank fastening, all the others are clinker with overlapping edges; the older types are sewn or laced, those of Björke-Hille and Nydam are riveted. All vessels of these finds had inserted single-part ribs, which were fastened to projecting sections of the planks.

Such a survey permits a clear answer to the question of the prototypes for the bronze age evolution of northern European shipbuilding. The unity of the way in which the shells have been fabricated and the striking marks left by the hollowing process of the stem and bottom plank compel the conclusion that only the dugout canoe can have been the ancestral model. In either case bottom shell boats were the transitional stage. Influences which become evident during the further process of evolution do not come from the shipbuilding technologies of the antique Mediterranean and Near-Eastern civilizations. The fact that the planks are sewn together, and the mode of lashing the often very lightweight inserted ribs, hint at early influences from the circumpolar technology of frame construction—influences which find their explanation in cultural contacts of the middle stone age.

Maritime cultural history has long explored the origins of framed and planked ship construction, which became, from the 16th century on, the determining technique for European shipbuilding. Formerly the view prevailed that the home of frame construction was to be sought in the Mediterranean. The Mediterranean wreck finds contradict this theory, which was based on the erroneous supposition that flush-sided or carvel planking is identical with frame construction as such. After it had been unmistakably established that in the antique classical civilizations ships were built using shell construction technology, it should be clear that we must look for the origin of planked frame construction in those regions where age-old traditions of popular frame construction have remained intact to the present, by which we mean the continued making of prototypical skin-covered boats. In Europe, this is the case only in the area of Wales, Ireland and Scotland.

Let us now check the familiar historical sources attesting to the introduction of the frame type of construction in the realm of the cities of the Hanse. In Zealand and Holland a beginning was made in 1459 with the construction of carvel-built ships under the direction of a Breton master builder. In 1460 the Dutch town of Hoorn followed suit; in the chronicles of this town a quite unequivocal statement is found to the effect that this undertaking involved a "different manner of work": the side planks were not laid clinker-style and riveted one to the other, but flush and not fastened to one another, with a seam between planks. It is a lucky coincidence that exactly in 1460 a census of ships in the Schelde river was taken, according to which there were moored in the river at that time 44 "kraweels" of this type. Of these, 41 came from Brittany, the rest from Normandy, Scotland and northern Spain. In the Mediterranean, vessels of this kind were characteristically referred to as "Bretons" or "Bertons".

All this had already been pointed out by Bernhard Hagedorn by 1914. Equally well known was Julius Caesar's description of the ships of the Veneti in Northwest Gaul: "Their keel is flatter than that of the Roman ships. They are entirely built of oak. Their ribs, made of timber a foot thick, are fastened together with iron nails as thick as a man's thumb." And the Greek geographer Strabo, a little later, made this addition: "They are built of oak timber. However, instead of joining the side planks closely together, they leave open seams between them, which are caulked with seaweed." We are certain that the Celtic seagoing ships described by Caesar and Strabo were at that time built according to the same technology as the Breton kraweels of 1460.

Conclusive archeological proof that northwestern European frame construction with planks is older than previously supposed was produced in 1962. In this year Peter Marsden excavated in London the remains of a coastal freighter dating, as was incontrovertibly established by coins and pottery, from the 2nd century A.D. It is a sailing vessel, entirely of oak, a shoal-draft model of a bottom-plank boat. The carvel-laid side planks were fastened to the 12-inch ribs with iron nails as thick as a thumb; the seams were caulked with hazel leaves. No doubt remains now that at the period of the Roman conquest of Gaul and Britain framed construction was practiced over a large area, this being equally true for skin-covered and for planked vessels.

Words like *kraweel*, *carvel*, *caravela* are in use in Portuguese, Spanish, northern French and English dialects to designate ships, and, as is to be noted, originally small vessels, as well as pannier-like baskets. The term *carvel* thus does not designate the technique of flush-sided plank joining but the frame construction itself, as manifested in primitive basketmaking as well as in certain kinds of boats.

The center whence innovations in the European modes of framed and planked construction radiated, must be sought, for the pre-Roman times, in the maritime regions bordered by the Bay of Biscay, Brittany and Scotland. It is not unthinkable that this important development has a connection with the bronze age ore-carrying sea trade between England, Ireland and Asturia and thus constitutes an outcome of contacts with the ancient maritime cultures of the Mediterranean area.

Right:
Richly decorated ceremonial paddles from Polynesia.

The Deep-water Vessel

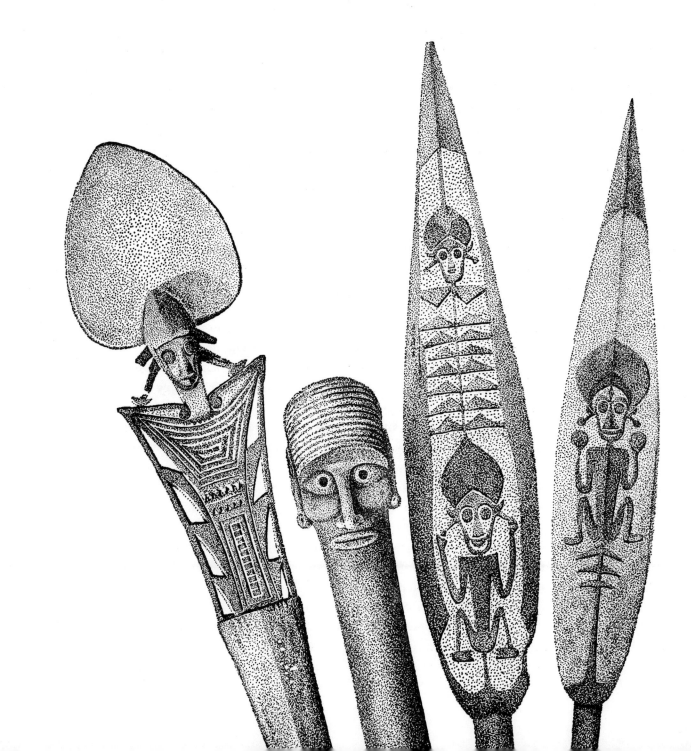

Technical Innovations in the Orient

The era of long voyages across broad ocean tracts began in the eastern Mediterranean and the Persian Gulf with the bronze age. Trading ventures to shores as distant as Britain and Scandinavia, the Azores and the Canary Islands, to South India and East Africa were made, of which we hear last echoes in Homer's poetry and in the seafaring myths of antiquity.

Millennia after this prelude fresh impulses emanated from the coastal countries of the Indian Ocean and the Southeast Asian maritime region, where essential technical innovations in navigation had taken place. The writings on natural history of the Roman Plinius of the 1st century, the first sailing manual or directory for the Indian Ocean dating a little later and written in Egyptian Alexandria, the "Periplus Mare Erythräi" as well as statements from the Indian Sanskrit literature and from ancient Chinese chronicles, lastly some representations of ships in ancient Indian art, are all in accord respecting a revolutionary improvement of ship propulsion under sail: the introduction of rigs comprising several masts and fore-and-aft sails set parallel to the longitudinal axis of the hull. This new rig consists of sails shaped as vertical quadrilaterals trimmed in asymmetrical balance, wherein the area of maximum forward thrust, i.e. the windward leech, the edge pointing into the wind, is situated before the mast. A "lugsail" of this kind makes it possible to point as much as 20° closer to the wind direction. But the optimal aerodynamic effect is achieved only where the rig consists of more than one mast.

The two-master of the 2nd or 3rd century which appears on the coins of the Central Indian kingdom of Andhra shows, for the first time, what this innovation looked like. The three-masted ship from the mural paintings of the Indian temple of Ajanta (ill. 44), dateable about the 5th century, confirms the new type, as does a Sanskrit text which even speaks of four-masters. Plinius and the "Periplus" report that ships of this class were large seagoing craft of a cargo capacity of up to 3000 amphoras. The most precise data are given by a Chinese chronicler of the 3rd century: "The people who live to the south of the frontiers rig their ships, depending on their size, occasionally with as many as four sails, which are arranged in a peculiar way fore and aft. In this southern country there are trees with leaves more than a yard long. These are woven together for making the sails. The four sails are not arranged, as is customary, facing forward, but are placed slantingly to receive the wind. The wind inflates them at the after parts and is thus cast back from one sail to the next, so that they all benefit from the propelling force. Because this slanting position permits one sail to receive the breeze from the other, the worry arising from too tall a rig is ended. Thus it happens that these ships sail without avoiding gales, which makes very quick passages possible." Only a little later another writer states that there are nowadays ships which "bore their way into the wind". Their sails, it is said, are fitted so as to swing around the mast like a door around its hinges.

We do not know whether the invention of the fore-and-aft rig with several masts is to be placed in India or in some other country of the early feudal Orient. It is probable that several centers of innovation existed, among others the Pontic-Aegean region, whence corresponding pictorial representations from the 1st and 2nd centuries have come to us, and likewise the maritime region of Southeast Asia. In these parts, original types in temporary use, which could be set either parallel to the longitudinal axis or at right angles to it, were developed into variations of the spritsail, rigged unilaterally abaft the mast; empirical experimentation with the traditional square sail, set from a yard at right angles to the keel, led to a variety of forms of the lugsail, rigged parallel to the keel and extending abaft as well as forward of the mast.

54 Seagoing (Indian?) ship with lug rig. Detail from a relief of the temple of Buddha of Borobudur, Java, approximately 700.

55 *Vessel with outrigger under sail of the island of Ceylon.*

56 Japanese sailing trawler.

57 Figurative stem decoration of a chief's canoe from New Georgia, Solomon Islands, Melanesia.

58 Ritual ceramic bowl, with raft model, from the Peruvian pre-Inca coastal civilization Mochica III, about 600 to 800, now in the museum of Lima-Miraflores.

"The vessels built at Ormus are of the worst kind, and dangerous for navigation... Their defects proceed from the circumstance of nails not being employed in the construction, the wood being of too hard a quality and liable to split or crack like earthenware... The planks are bored, as carefully as possible, with an iron auger, near the extremities; and wooden pins or treenails being driven into them, they are in this manner fastened. After this they are bound, or rather sewed together, with a kind of rope-yarn stripped from the husks of the Indian nuts, which are of a large size, and covered with fibrous stuff like horsehair. This being steeped in water until the softer parts putrefy, the threads or strings remain clean, and of these they make twine for sewing the planks, which lasts long under water. Pitch is not used for preserving the bottoms of vessels, but they are smeared with an oil made from the fat of fish... The vessel has no more than one mast, one helm and one deck."

Marco Polo:
Die Reisen
(end of 13th century)
from: The Travels of Marco Polo,
revised from Marsden's translation
and edited by Manuel Komroff
The Modern Library, New York

Relics of both prototypes and of many regional transitional forms have been preserved in the maritime area between Ceylon and New Guinea. In the Gulf of Tonkin is to be sought the center of origin of the most perfect of all the variations of the Oriental lug rig. A noteworthy line of demarcation divides to this day the standing lug with its tack fastened to the mast from that of the balance lug with a free-swinging tack, the latter beginning north of Hué in Vietnam. The ingeniously calculated jet action of the three to five masts, some of which are stepped out of line with the keel of the ship, and the multiplication of the aerodynamic foil effect of the sails, which are divided by bamboo battens into narrow sections and can be swung in a full circle, make this so-called junk rig the most sophisticated of all sailing ship types (ill. 28e, 76).

Next to the lug rig the invention of the balanced rudder, joined to the stern and adjustable in its height of operation, improved the sailing qualities of vessels of the feudal Oriental cultures. This innovation has been documented for Chinese sailing craft since the 12th century. Indian, Persian and Arabian ships in later periods were fitted with axial rudders in fixed juncture with the hull. The invention seems to have had its origin in the *yuloh*, a sculling and steering oar carried loosely over the stern beams of older Chinese boats.

A relief in the Indian Buddhist sanctuary of Santchi shows a small boat with side planks sewn together and a three-man crew. This picture has been dated in the 2nd century. We see in it the oldest iconographical testimonial of a building technique known and practiced to this day in the ocean areas of the Orient, having dominated all other methods for ages. Again and again Europeans as well as Chinese have expressed astonishment at its use, especially in the large trading and official state vessels of Arabs, Indians, Malayans and Polynesians. By itself the method of sewing planks, bark slabs or animal hides together for boat hull coverings has worldwide distribution, being encountered in Africa (ill. 152), Asia, Oceania and America. But only in the waters between Madagascar and Polynesia, with the center of origin located in the Malayan-Indonesian region, was this method, first developed by the lowly toilers of the sea, adapted to the building of ships for the ruling classes.

Another invention in boat design of seafarers and fishermen, the twin-hulled boat, rose from popular ranks to the levels of Far Eastern class cultures. A permanent parallel junction of two dugouts or bottom shell boats by means of transverse beams, surmounted by a crew and cargo-carrying platform, produces nearly capsize-proof vessels of great deadweight capacity. We know the small versions of such types from South China, the middle Mekong, the Ganges and Ceylon. But the greatest perfection of these vessels is reached in the large blue-water craft of Oceania, from the Carolines to Hawaii, Tahiti and New Zealand (ill. 59). They were brought to these regions by migrations emanating from Southeast Asia. The spectacle of these oceangoing vessels of a length of up to 40 meters and capable of carrying crews of 200 to 300 men, rushing through the water on their twin keels caused the greatest admiration among the Europeans on the voyages of discovery of the 17th and 18th centuries. Their crab-claw rig, a regional variant of the fore-and-aft rig, drove them along faster than three-masted frigates.

59 Twin-hull boat from the Tonga Islands in Polynesia.
From: Jacob LeMaire, Ephemerides sive descriptio navigationes
australis anno 1615, Amsterdam 1622.
The figure of a cock in the sail is the oldest known iconographical
and ornamental boat decoration in Oceania.

Georg Forster, who participated in James Cook's second South Sea
expedition as scientist, confirmed in 1773 that the Tonganese wove
figures of turtles or of cocks into their sails, probably as symbols of
earlier totemistic cults. Branches and bird feathers were used to
decorate the mast trucks.

Long-distance Voyages
in the Indian and Pacific Oceans

At about the beginning of our era, great numbers of Indian ships departed annually for Southeast Asia. In the wake of the sailors came merchants, missionaries, and adventurers belonging to the upper castes, who settled and became active in the new countries. The indigenous aristocratic classes of some of the Southeast Asian commonwealths gradually adopted the Indian civilization imported fom across the sea, to an extent where one could speak of "Hinduized" states, where Hinduism, Buddhism, Sanskrit and Indian art were appreciated as much as among the ruling classes of India. In most of these states navigation had the dignity of a civic trade and played a dominant role.

In this evolutionary process the kingdom of Funan, situated in the delta and the lower basin of the Mekong, seems to have had a leading part, creating for itself a lucrative mediating position in overseas trade and cultural exchanges. In 1963 the report of the protracted excavations of the ruins of the former seaport of Oc-éo, once a capital town of Funan, was published. The archeologists had come upon extensive pile works and breakwaters; astonishing quantities of Indian, Persian and Greco-Roman coins, jewelry and cult objects belonging to nearly all the civilizations between Mediterranean and Pacific were found. Remnants of ships were not among the finds, which was no more than was expected. But the representations of ships in the reliefs of the world-famous temple pyramids of Borobudur in Java (ill. 54) and Angkor in Cambodia, which are counted among the most significant architectural achievements of the Hinduized cultures, give us an idea, nevertheless, of the principal types of vessels in use around the period, and of their advanced sailing technique. They were capacious, large freighters, fore-and-aft rigged with more than one mast.

60 Daggerboards of Peruvian rafts of the Inca period (after Dieter Eisleb).

In primitive societies and in early feudal civilizations outside of Europe, the means of propulsion and steering of vessels of importance in communal affairs were often ornamented. The handles and blades of paddles, and the handles of the daggerboards that were used for steering log rafts, were preferred places for decoration.

During the second half of the 1st millennium A.D. at the latest, seagoing tribes had departed from the maritime area between South China and Celebes in several migratory waves, moving in a southeasterly direction towards Oceania. A first stage was reached in the islands of the Fiji, Samoa and Tonga groups; subsequent thrusts launched from these centers carried the migrants thousands of miles farther into the Pacific: to New Zealand, Hawaii and Easter Island, possibly as far as the west coast of America. In their double-hulled boats up to 40 meters long, carrying the aerodynamically superlatively effective crab-claw rig, they were even able to sail through the zone of perpetual gales in the latitudes of the roaring forties and reached, in the 7th century, the limits of the antarctic icepack.

About the year 550 the kingdom of Shrividshaja had come into being in Indonesia on the island of Sumatra. It was a Hindu state with pronounced maritime activity.

Malayan sailors spread their techniques of ship construction, e.g. the outrigger type, across the ocean to Madagascar and Somalia. In the seaport towns of Mogadishu, Lamu, Malindi, Mombasa, Pemba, Zanzibar and Kilwa, whose origins date to this period, Bantu-African, Arabic, Indian and Malayan elements were fused into the pre-Islamic Suaheli culture, the archeological study of which has only recently begun. In the excavations of ancient Kilwa, coins from Rome, Byzantium, Persia and Mesopotamia were found; Siamese stoneware was reposing side by side with Chinese porcelain and Indian cut glassware; amber, pearls, ivory figurines and jewelry of jade and copper were also found. Under the expansion of Islamic civilization, the Arabic character of these seaport cities later increased. But until their destruction by the Portuguese (1502) the maritime culture of East Africa continued to be a conglomerate of Suaheli, Arabic and Hindu elements.

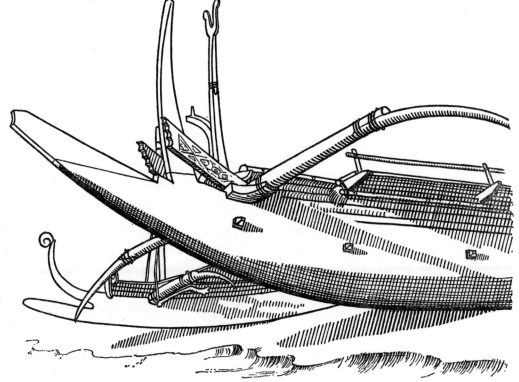

61 Forked stem of an Indonesian proa (after W. O. J. Nieuwenkamp). The ethnographers Wilhelm Müller-Wismar and Christian Nooteboom have speculated that the fork-shaped stem construction of many vessels of Southeast Asia and Oceania, with traces extending as far as Alaska, and which cannot be satisfactorily explained on functional grounds, may have originated as a cultic symbol. The incurving snail- or fiddlehead at the tip of the cutwater of many Indian vessels may well have a similar origin. Below this carving, which is called surul, *is a compartment for the keeping of the objects used in the magic ceremonials observed during the voyage: conch shell, incense container and oil lamp.*

Saracens and Italian Maritime Cities

In the European portion of the Mediterranean, the Arabic-Islamic expansion of the 7th and 8th centuries changed the maritime picture which had existed since the flowering of the Roman Empire. Within a short time the Moslem Saracens became the rulers over the western Mediterranean basin. Their principal strongholds were in North Africa and southern Spain. Further thrusts met with bitter resistance on the part of the maritime cities of Barcelona, Marseilles, Genoa and Venice, all of which were reaping profits from overseas trade (ill. 89). Their opportunity came when, in the 12th century, the Christian feudal rulers urgently needed a powerful fleet for troop transport and supplies for the Crusades against the Islamic countries of the Levant. Bids made by the cities, which are preserved, give us an idea of the medieval Mediterranean heavy freighters which carried up to 500 tons deadweight and were 30 meters long. In contrast to the single-masted square-riggers of the Imperium Romanum, the "Navi" from the maritime cities of Italy, Provence and Catalonia had two or three masts and carried huge, triangular lateen sails, laced to long yards rigged parallel to the longitudinal axis of the ship, slanted upward and aft (ill. 87). No exact information concerning the origin and early evolution of the lateen rig in the Mediterranean is available at the present time. The oldest pictorial documents showing the rig come from northern Aegean tombstone reliefs of the 1st and 2nd centuries, and Greek miniatures of the 9th century.

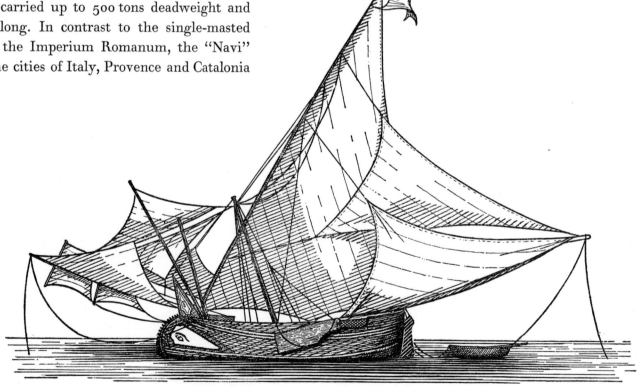

62 *Muleta on the Tagus (after Cecil Trew).*
This sailing fisherman of the Tagus estuary exceeds all the other curious types of the Portuguese coastal waters in bizarreness of rig. Sailing before the wind, it tows a dragnet fastened to outrigger poles.

The only sea trade in northern Europe at all comparable to that of the Mediterranean was carried on from the Atlantic coast. Here, after the waning of the Roman rule, there had been no interruption of marine enterprises, which continued to be pursued both on the routes to Brittany, Ireland and Scotland, and southward to the country of the Basques and Asturia. After consolidation of the early feudal empire of the Franks in the 6th and 7th centuries, the field of operations of the maritime Franks and of the equally ancient Friesian sea trade enlarged, to extend at last throughout the coastal regions from the Bay of Biscay to the Baltic. The merchantmen of the Basques, Bretons, Franks and Friesians and of their correspondents relied on ports of call such as San Sebastian, Bayonne, La Rochelle, London, Schleswig and Birka on the shore of Lake Mälar in Sweden. From the southern Baltic coast, Wolin on the Oderhaff and the Prussian Truso on the Nogat delta entered into this network of early medieval sea trade routes, the principal cargoes being woolen cloth from Flanders, cutlery, Gallic wine, articles of luxury from the Levant and pelts from the Baltic.

The typology of the predominant freighter of these times, the nef, sailing from the Atlantic and Channel ports, has been the object of contention among scholars. It seems likely that they were heavy cargo sailers with side steering oar, carrying a single-masted square rig. Many were probably built in the frame method, which would mean that there was an essential difference of construction between them and the Germanic and Mediterranean types.

In the North the period from 800 to 1100 is considered to be the time of the Vikings or Normans. Curiously erroneous concepts are often connected with these names, which is hardly surprising in view of the still numerous gaps in information concerning essential aspects of the civilization of these centuries, despite numerous earth finds and voluminous chronicled tradition (ill. 65). It must be that the Viking rovers, but no less also the contemporary Slavic, Baltic and Finnish traders in the Baltic, as well as Croats, Dalmatians and Saracens in the Mediterranean, brought good as well as bad with them, constructing here, devastating there, and were instruments of civilization as readily as of inhuman destruction. All these peoples lived during a period of upheaval: the dissolution of the traditional rule of the Gentiles and of the customs and religious creeds characterizing their era. New social concepts and industries were coming on the scene everywhere. The ambivalent evaluation associated with the maritime enterprise of the Vikings can therefore be seen as a typical expression of the transition to feudalism.

However this may be, the Norman voyages are most impressive achievements, which remained unequalled for centuries. They doubled the North Cape and explored the White Sea, made deep thrusts into the south and sailed in 859 through the Straits of Gibraltar to the coast of Italy.

In eastern Europe their extensive river voyages carried them by way of the Neva, Volkhov and Volga to the Caspian Sea, via the Dnieper to the Black Sea. They crossed the stormy North Atlantic, sailing in their open boats thousands of miles to Greenland and thence, around the year 1000, to the American coast, which they named Vinland. Viking settlements were excavated in 1962 in Newfoundland.

Swedish Vikings founded around 860, in the border territories between Finnish and Slavonic tribal settlements, an establishment on the shore of Lake Ilmen, which was destined to grow into a trade center of European dimensions, the mighty mercantile republic of Novgorod.

Many ship finds from Scandinavia present us with an idea of what the Viking vessels looked like (ill. 63, 65, 66). The most precise information comes from the salvaging of five wrecks from the Danish Roskildefjord (ill. 67) by Ole Crumlin, completed in 1968. Viking freighters were built in dimensions ranging from 10 to 25 meters overall length, uniformly belonging to the class of clinker-built keelboat with open cargo space, rigged with a single mast carrying a square sail. The bottom plank of the Scandinavian prototype was gradually developed into a T-shaped timber keel by the later shipbuilders through a progressive accentuation of the vertical dimension. The gouging signs at fore and after ends gradually disappeared. The inserted ribs were made in several sections and no longer lashed together but nailed to the side planking. The trial voyage with the replica of the Gokstad boat, in which Captain Anderson sailed from Norway to New York in 1893 in four weeks, demonstrated anew the seaworthiness of the Viking craft. However, their modest cargo capacity of 10 to 20 tons does not bear comparison to the Mediterranean freighters.

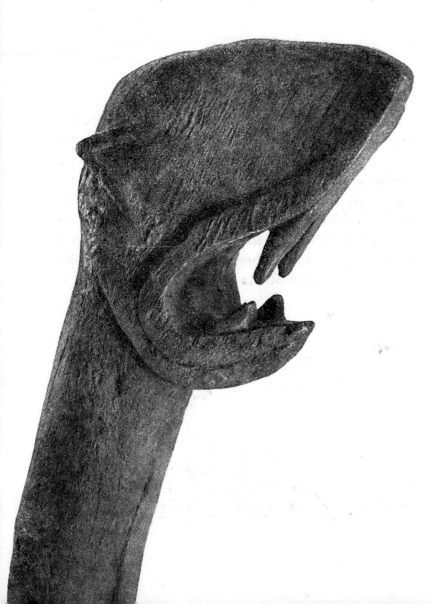

63 This stem ornament in form of a dragon's head was dredged up from the Schelde and probably belonged to a Viking ship which foundered in the 9th century. It is thought that carvings of this kind were anti-sorcery devices, besides having the more immediate function of striking an adversary with terror.

64 *Norwegian rock murals with representations of ships. Since the late stone age, we find in the rock pictures of northern Europe, Siberia and Alaska, as well as in the rock engravings of Nubia and the rock paintings of New Guinea, representations of ships, either singly or in groups and often in conjunction with human or animal figures. The Scandinavian and Nubian rock mural representations of ships have been the subject of passionate discussions of the vehicles that may have been the models for these works of art. However, these rock pictures must not be viewed as technical drawings nor as historical, pictorial chronicles. They evidently belong to the category of symbols of cultic concepts of primeval society, possibly constituting a hunting magic, possibly reflecting a cult of spirit worship, perhaps of sun worship.*

GOKSTADSKIBET

Left: 65 The Gokstad ship, excavated on the west shore of the Oslo fjord. This Viking vessel dates from about 850 and is exhibited in the museum of Bygdøy near Oslo.

66 Gilded so-called "ship's wind vane" of the Viking period, about 950, from the Swedish Province of Hälsingland. The device probably had a magical or ceremonial function.

Since the bronze age, several religions had pronouncedly maritime funerary traditions, obviously stemming from the belief that those who have died must cross a sea or broad river to some distant shore, in order to reach the Land of the Dead. Concepts connected with this belief were different in the various civilizations and underwent frequent changes. As an example, we cite the Scandinavian custom of the 9th century, of burying notable military leaders or kings with their dependents, on shore in large ships measuring as much as 20 meters or more, fully provisioned and otherwise supplied with equipment for the imagined journey to the Land of the Dead: horse and carriage, sleigh, tent and kitchen utensils. The most splendid northern ship entombments discovered are those at Oseberg and Gokstad.

Left: 67 Prow of the Viking ship wreck No. 3 from Skuldelev in the Danish Roskilde fjord, dateable about 1000. For salvage purposes, the water has been drained off.

68 A portion of the early feudal period shipwreck of Slavic origin from the Baltic Sea, found at Ralswiek on the island of Rügen, DDR, in 1967.

The boats of the Slavic tribes which had penetrated into the southern Baltic area during the age of the migrations differed from the Scandinavian vessels in a feature of construction common to all Slavic wreck finds from Warnemünde and Rügen, Szczecin and Wolin to the mouth of the Leba and the bay of Gdánsk: their clinker-laid planks were fastened with treenails, not riveted together.

69 *During dredging operations in the Weser near Bremen in 1962, an ancient large wreck was discovered and identified as a kogge by the staff of the Bremen Focke Museum. It was salvaged after a great deal of labor. This ship goes back to the end of the 14th century.*

Right: 70 *This beautiful* **Koggensiegel** *(kogge seal) was ordered by the Hanse town of Stralsund (granted city privileges in 1234) to be engraved for its uses during the 14th century. The devices on city seals with their (largely accurate) figures of seagoing merchant ships typical of the time, had become since the end of the 12th century (emanating from the French maritime trading cities) the representative sign of cultivation, prosperity and power of the leading classes of citizens of the seaport cities during the flourishing of feudalism.*

71 The "Catalan Nao" of the Rotterdam Maritiem Museum, "Prins
Hendrik" by name, a work of the
early 15th century, is believed to be
the oldest ship model thus far known.
It is likely that it was originally a
votive offering to the Sailors' Chapel
of Mataró in Catalonia. The single-
masted, square-rigged nao typefies
the cargo sailer of the 14th century
of western and southern Europe.

72 Ship models like this masterpiece of silversmithing of Parisian origin from the end of the 15th century, now in the Victoria & Albert Museum in London, were used as symbolic table ornaments at the feudal royal courts.

A new type of cargo carrier of significantly greater dead-weight capacity developed only from the 12th century on in the North Sea and Baltic regions. Since the maritime Crusades this kind of ship was generally known as the Friesian and Low German troop transport, under the name of *Heer Kogge* or *Herren Kogge*. After 1200 this designation begins to appear in various archives of places ranging from the Baltic coast to the Basque country and to Marseilles. It is possible that the feature, new in Europe, of the axial stern rudder—probably a Friesian or Flemish invention of the late 12th century—was rated a criterion of this class of vessel, which for more than 200 years came to represent the bulk cargo carrier par excellence in the sea trade of the Flemish-Friesian ports and of the Low German union of coastal towns of the Hanse. But square-riggers referred to as *Koggen* are also known from England, France, the seaport cities of the Basque Hermandad and Italy. Many scientists have made studies of the design, construction and building methods of this class of ship; the opinions frequently clash. Aside from conceding the rig and the novel steering technique, no satisfactory consensus has been reached to this date.

In October 1962 an ancient wreck was located in the Weser near Bremen, identified as a ship of the Hanse and presumed to be a Kogge (ill. 69). This find caused a sensation among naval historians. Salvage operations encountered difficulties, but notwithstanding the group of scientists working with Siegfried Fliedner succeeded in completing the task before winter set in.

The Kogge of Bremen proved to be a ship 24 meters long, 7 meters wide, of about 130 tons loading capacity. Typologically speaking it is an unusual vessel: a double-ended bottom plank ship with so-called "inside stem" and stern-post, the sides of both stem and stern timbers being covered by the side planking. The three lowermost plank strakes were carvel or flush laid, while the upper ones were laid clinker or lapstrake fashion. This find was

the hull of a newly built, not quite finished ship, which apparently was washed off the stocks of the municipal shipyard during some gale and drifted into a side branch of the Weser, where it stranded and sank. The oak timbers of the ship were dated as belonging to the time around 1380.

During the early growth phase of the maritime cities of northern Europe it had become possible to increase the cargo capacity of the standard freighters of the Kogge and Nef type to about 200 tons. This was the limit of what was feasible by the customary shell construction technology then in use in the yards of the German Hanse towns and Dutch and English builders. It seems logical that the shipbuilders of the coasts of Flanders and Holland, being the most advanced not only in the technical and economic sense but also in general awareness, should have been the first to show interest in adapting to their uses the technique of frame construction practiced in western Europe. Caravels built in this manner in the yards of Portugal, northern Spain, Brittany and Normandy had been seen frequently, especially in Bruges, the seaport of worldwide trade in the 14th century, where ships from Italy and Castile had occasion to encounter those of the German Hanse, and of the English and Scandinavians. In Flanders yards had probably begun to build kraweels around 1440 or earlier. In 1459 a Breton master builder constructed in Holland the first vessel in the "changed manner of work" which, unless it had already been used previously without much publicity, was to spread during the last decades of the 15th century with uncommon rapidity through the entire maritime area that had been the stronghold of lapstrake construction. The reason for this was that the time was ripe for economic and cultural developments, not the least of which was, where the northern European seaport cities are concerned, the building of larger freighters of a burthen of 500 to 600 tons. The timing and manner of introduction of the frame construction method in the Mediterranean is a problem not yet clarified. In the chronicles of the city of Florence occurs a curious and ambiguous statement to the effect that at the beginning of the 14th century there was "a great change in maritime affairs". Basque ships from Bayonne are said to have given the impulse for this: vessels which the chronicler refers to as *cocche* (Kogge), and of which he states that the cost of building is less than the method then in use in Italy. Can this mean that the Basques, who had no equals in sailing achievement, helped to propagate the northern style of shell construction of the Koggen—which sounds sufficiently improbable—or are we here confronted with an unclear piece of information referring to the introduction of the technology of frame construction, whose chief characteristic, the series use of prefabricated frame moulds, undoubtedly did lower the cost of ship construction?

Be that as it may, clinker-built vessels went rapidly out of fashion in northern Europe for deep-sea voyages. However, in 1587 a clinker-built ship still formed part of John Davis' arctic expedition in search of the northwest passage between Canada and Greenland. This ship leaked so badly at times that the crew had to pump up to 300 strokes an hour. In Davis' journal a nautical invention then of recent origin, ordinary but rarely honored with a mention, is documented: the ship's pump. This instrument begins to appear in archival reports in the second half of the 15th century. Previously, water that leaked into a hull had to be thrown out by means of bailers, buckets and winnowing shovels. Sailors will be able to appreciate the vital importance of the innovation.

The same 15th century brought another important advance in the evolution of sailing technique for deep-sea vessels. Beginning in Brittany, England and the Netherlands, the sailors of the period developed the type of three-masted vessel which has remained the standard until the present, wherein the area of the square sails on fore and main mast was subdivided, first into two, soon after 1500 into three sails (ill. 28b). Henceforth it was possible to set above the large courses (fore and main sails) smaller topsails and topgallant sails, the aftermost or mizzen mast continuing to carry a lateen sail. Wholly typical of the spirit of the times in this century of early capitalist sea-going technology is the fact that the chronicles of the Dutch seaport cities give for the first time the name of the inventor of a nautical improvement together with an account of the innovation: the burgher and shipmaster Kryn Wouters thought out the extension of masts by means of a division into a lower mast and a removable or "housing" spar above it, the topmast.

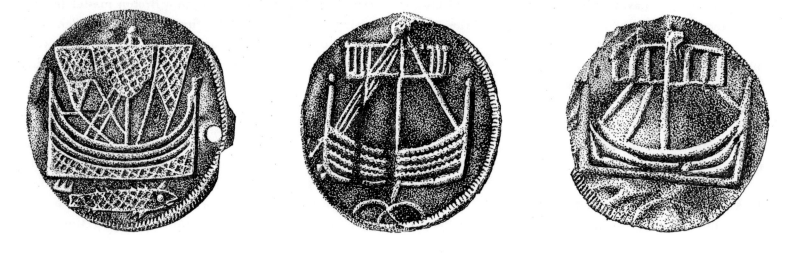

ARCHA·NOB

habitatio mũ aialium habitatio hoĩm habitatio ĩ mũ aialium

Apotheca herbarum Apotheca specierum

Stercoraria

73 Left: The denarii struck in the 8th–9th century in the Frankish, Friesian and Scandinavian seaport settlements of Quentovik, Dorestad and Birka (or Haithabu) showed the "Great Ship" symbol for the first time; it was a sign of civic international mercantile activity, a social stratum then in the act of forming (after Siegfried Fliedner).

74 The marine motifs of the Bible—the building of Noah's ark, the immolation of the prophet Jonah, St. Peter casting the net, the shipwreck of the Apostle Paul—were favorite subjects in early Christian art from the Byzantine period on. The earliest of such illustrations were in hand-painted miniatures. After 1450 the first printed Bibles and cosmographies were illustrated and decorated with woodcuts of this kind of subject matter. Our example shows the building of Noah's ark in the "Weltchronik" of the humanist Hartmann Schedel of 1493.

Warhaffte Contrafactur/ der Herzlichen gewaltigen vnnd
wolgerüsten grossen Venedischen Galleen/ zum gebrauch vnd Schlachten des Meers:
Newlich eygentlich entworffen vnnd verfertigt/ sampt aller jr zugehör/ für alle die jenigen/ so weyt vnnd ferz des Meers erkandtnus nit bewüst/ sich deren erlustigen zusehen/
Welche diß 1 5 7 1. Jar/ wider den Erbfeind der Christenheit des Türcken/ zugerichtet/ gemacht vnnd gebraucht worden/ deren sie in jrer Schlacht/ sechß zum angriff voran geschickt/ vnd dermassen mit jrem grossen Geschütz/ so gewaltig vnd wolgetroffen/
volgendts mit jrem nachdruck/ durch gnad vnd beystand deß Allmechtigen Gottes/ die Victorj vnd
Syg erhalten.

75 After the invention of printing with movable letter types, accounts of the sea voyages of the Portuguese, Spaniards and French were quickly disseminated through Europe from the late 15th century on. Illustrated broadsides announced events as they became known. Our illustration shows the title page of a pamphlet describing the naval battle of Lepanto—the last naval engagement in history in which rowing ships were used—on the west coast of Greece, where, in 1571, the galleys and galleasses of the allied Venetians and Spaniards vanquished the Turkish navy.

Right:
76 Chinese junk of the 18th century. Illustration from Johann Hinrich Röding's "Wörterbuch der Marine", published at Hamburg 1794–1798. The first special dictionaries of nautical terms began to appear about the middle of the 17th century in England, France and the Netherlands.

The large seagoing ship of Europe had been nearly perfected as a type by 1450. The achievements of the European navigators in these vessels belong to common knowledge.

From Lisbon to Novgorod, from Bergen to Dubrovnik, the aim of the early capitalist class of entrepreneurs of the urban bourgeoisie was to secure direct trade connections with the legendary markets of the East, collectively referred to as "India". But the ruling feudal lords of Europe—emperors, popes, kings and princes—were equally interested in adding new ways of increasing their private fortunes and bank accounts, competing in this aim with shipowners and great merchant firms and manufactories in the European centers of industry. The interests of these social classes were met halfway by the ambitions of some hundred daring and enterprising sea captains, dreaming of achieving greater things with their commands than humdrum coastal navigation. Here and there such urges were added to by humanistic scholars desiring to explore the unknown.

Under this singular concordance of interests, sails were hoisted for long-distance voyages to unexplored oceans

BALZE DE GUAYAQUIL dans toutes ses proportions.

A. la Proue.
B. la Poupe.
C. la Ramée ou Cabane.
D. Perche qui sert de Mât.
E. Bouline.
F. Bigues.
G. Rame qui sert de Boussole et de Gouvernail.
H. Cuisine.
I. Bouteilles d'aigue.
K. Haubans.
L. Barbacoa ou Couvert.

BALSA oder FAHRZEUG VON GUAYAQUIL mit seinen Verhaeltnissen vorgestellet.

A. Das Vordertheil.
B. Das Hindertheil.
C. Die Laube oder Hütte.
D. Stangen welche statt des Mastes dienen
E. Segelleinen.
F. Schutzhoelzer.
G. Ruder, welches zum Schutzholze und Steuerruder dienet.
H. Die Küche.
I. Wasserflaschen.
K. Haupttauen oder die Wand.
L. Der Boden oder das Bedeck.

77 Seagoing, square-rigged balsa log raft from Peru.
From: George Juan et Antoine de Ulloa, Voyage de l'Amérique méridionale, Amsterdam 1752

Right:
78 Log raft (under fore-and-aft sail) from the Polynesian Gambiera Islands, after a drawing made by Captain Beechey (1825).
From: F. W. Beechey, Narrative of a Voyage to the Pacific, London 1831. Many of the European navigators of the age of discoveries witnessed vessels like these with astonishment and the honest admiration due to fellow professionals. On the basis of their often very detailed descriptions and sketches copper engravings were made which gave Europeans the first authentic illustrations of vessels from India, Southeast Asia, China, Oceania and America.

from Portugal, Spain, France, England and the Netherlands. The boldest of the adventurers steered a westerly course straight across the Atlantic. Columbus sailed along the latitude of the Tropic of Cancer. Cabot, Cartier, Frobisher, Davis, Hudson and Baffin tried to reach the goal by the devious route of a northwest passage at the border of the arctic. Vespucci and Magellan attacked the problem of the passage to India by traversing the Atlantic on a southwesterly course. Barents hoped to unlock the northeast passage along the Siberian coast. Diaz chose the southeast route along the coasts of Africa. Pushing ahead on the same course, da Gama was the first to reach the promised land of India. Twenty years later, Portuguese ships entered the harbor of Canton, a few years later that of Nagasaki. Magellan had the unheard-of ambition to circumnavigate the globe. He did not live to see it done, but a portion of his crew under the command of the Basque d'Elcano accomplished it. Drake was the second to carry through this gigantic feat of navigation. All these first, world-spanning voyages were executed in the 150 years between 1470 and 1620.

Maritime Historiography

The glory gained in these fortunate voyages of discovery shed its glamor on the splendid ships that had brought the adventurers safely home again. The gold and silver-bearing galleons, fleuts and frigates began to be viewed with covetous eyes by the feudal lords. The interest shown in maritime affairs by the ruling classes stimulated the humanists of the bourgeoisie to study the history and technique of navigation. In 1536 the first work of this kind was published in Paris, the "Annotationes de re navali" written in Latin by Lazare Baif. Bartolomeo Crescentio printed the "Nautica Mediterranea" in 1601 in Rome. The first corresponding German work to appear was the "Architectura navalis" by the councillor Joseph Furttenbach of Ulm (1629). The "Hydrographie" by the Jesuit Father Georges Fournier (Paris 1643) had encyclopedic significance. The profusely illustrated volume "Aeloude en hedendaegsche Scheep Bouw" by Nicolaes Witsen of Amsterdam (1671) has become a classic. In 1697 a professional was heard from for the first time, the master shipbuilder Cornelis van Yk of Delft, in his book "De Nederlandsche Scheepsbouwkonst open gestelt".

79 *A twin-hulled boat with oarsmen in battle masks from Hawaii. From: James Cook,* Voyage to the Pacific, *London 1785, 2nd ed. The voyages of discovery of the Portuguese, Spaniards, French, Britons and Dutch were responsible for the printing of cosmographies as well as for the engravings of the first European global maps.*

Magnificently illustrated accounts of these journeys testified to the contribution made in the knowledge of our world by those first captains of great voyages. Their logbooks told also of the fact that others, besides Europeans, were able to engage in successful ocean navigation.

The inclusion of ships as subjects in the contemporary art of the Renaissance approximately parallels the evolution of maritime historiography. Although artistic representations of ships and other vessels are found as early as late antiquity and the early Middle Ages—the gorgeous volume of plates of Friedrich Moll (1929) is an eloquent witness of this, as far as church frescoes and mosaics, reliefs, stained-glass windows and tapestries are concerned, also examples of early Christian book decoration for collections of psalms, missals, popular theological works and clerical chronicles—there is a difference in emphasis. Even in cases where the vessels are carefully rendered and here and there may correspond to some existing model, in the Middle Ages they are hardly ever the central theme of a work of art, but are mostly used as accessories with the function of religious symbols.

The symbol of the ship was familiar to Christianity, since it corresponded to a traditional concept of antiquity. Nautical symbolism is inseparable from Greek and Roman literature. The ship as the symbol of a well-ordered community was regarded as an antique precursor. Logically the ship became the symbol of the church of Christ, and equally logically the configuration of mast and yard—the sign of the cross—became a symbol of salvation and good luck. The writings of the early church fathers list regular catalogs of maritime symbols for Christian elements of faith. According to them, Christ was the helmsman, storms meant false and heretic creeds, shipwreck stood for original sin. Most of the pictures of vessels in old religious art must be viewed from this symbolic aspect.

A first change came in the 8th century. The flowering of the sea trade of the Franks and Friesians, which began about this period, indicates a far-reaching shift in social conditions in the period of early European feudalism, marked by greater freedom for a broad stratum of tradesmen and artisans, as well as by new forms of the organization of work and generally increased economic productivity. In the wake of economic development followed a cultural upsurge, and in the specifically maritime culture of the coastal region of the empire of the Franks we find that, for the first time in northern Europe, the ship is represented as a profane symbol. Charlemagne chose the device of the contemporary standard cargo sailor for the minting of the denarii which were struck around the year 780 in his seaport towns of Dorestad in the Rhine delta, and Quentovik to the south of Calais (ill. 73). With this act the ship of long voyages was deliberately established as a symbol of emancipated trade activity. The novel image was soon imitated: prior to 850 there were already silver coins with designs of square-riggers in the Baltic area.

By the 12th century, several important European merchant cities, on the strength of their economic development and advanced social structure, had attained a political status which gave them, de jure or de facto, a position of sovereignty and put them on an equal footing with the powerful secular and clerical feudal rulers. This sovereignty secured for them the authority to conclude diplomatic treaties. To be legally binding, state contracts required an additional valliditating designation besides the signatures of the contracting powers: they had to be sealed. The feudal institutions chose devices for their seals which they deemed to be expressive of their way of life.

The French, English and German seaport towns, from the end of the 12th century on, had a square-rigger in their seals. Their example was followed by the German-speaking seaport towns founded in the territories of the Baltic Slavs, Balts and Estonians, and by many of the harbor settlements in Scandinavia (ill. 70). With this development, effigies of ships became a central theme in medieval art, no longer stemming from Christian dogma but from a realization of the social and political significance of urban identity, at that period a bearer of progress.

This civic society of skippers, shipbuilders and overseas merchants also liked to use ships in other connections, always very definitely as realistically rendered designs of their estate: in the carved work of church pews and nautical fraternities, in the chandeliers, candle holders and censers of guild donations. Ship models dating from this period are also known; they ornamented town halls, churches (ill. 71) and guild halls. Shipowners, merchants, the corporations of shipmasters and builders, had precious ship models made to their order, usually of silver, for table décor for festive banquets, herein imitating the feudal court custom (ill. 72).

In those regions where marine affairs were especially predominant a gradual change even in works devoted to sacred purposes becomes evident from the late 14th century on: the approach to the theme of the ship of the time changes from symbolism to realism; the object is depicted true to nature and becomes the central motif.

We may observe this process in certain paintings of saints from the coastal centers of the Netherlands and Lower Germany, and it can also be seen very clearly in the somewhat earlier works of the Venetian painters. Quite a few paintings, woodcuts and copper engravings from the period of 1450–1550 may almost be described as early examples of "marines". We are thinking of the works of Carpaccio, Bordone, van Eyck, Hieronymus Bosch and Pieter Breughel the Elder (ill. 82). A "marine" is a painting, drawing, etc. in which the theme is set by ships figuring either predominantly or exclusively in a composition, including a typical environment either of the open sea or the activities of a harbor, approached in a realistic manner. This branch of purely secular art emerged around the turn of the 16th century, most clearly marked in the Netherlands, where more than 80 artists devoted themselves to this genre in a single century. The best-known of the Dutch marine painters is Willem van de Velde the Younger, active from 1653–1707, but living in England after 1673 (ill. 83). Reinier Nooms' series of 36 copper engravings entitled "Various Ships of Amsterdam" is a superb work of marine graphics. Marine painting also flourished during the French baroque period.

80 An excess of ornamentation was displayed in the 18th century by the state barges of the feudal rulers of Southeast Asia, for instance the ritual vessels of the kings of Burma, Laos and Thailand. From: Choisy, Journal du voyage de Siam, Amsterdam 1688. For ages the annual regatta of such vessels on the Menam and Mekong rivers had been a part of ritualistic tradition in connection with the Buddhist feast at the termination of the rainy season. The regattas of the dragon boats of South China, at the feast of the summer solstice, were most impressive. In the 19th century, the dragon boats

Ballon du Roy à 120 Rameurs

were owned by the corporations. They were between 20 and 40 meters long, very narrow, built as double-ended plank boats, the largest of which were paddled by as many as sixty men. Their form, mode of construction and technique of propulsion combined to create an exceptionally old-fashioned effect. The gilded dragons' heads with flowing manes were fitted to the cutwater shortly before the start of the regatta. The stern terminated in a carved, scaly dragon's tail. The sides were painted blue, the waterline set off in vermilion. The name of the ship was embroidered on a burgee floating from the prow, for instance "Boat of the Hundred Masters". Behind the flagstaff stood the boat's captain, indicating the course to the paddlers. Midships were seated two men who beat time for the paddling on gong and bass drum. The helmsman stood on a platform at the stern. The regatta was over a course of 1500 meters. Start and finish were traditionally accompanied by ceremonial acts, such as casting rice in the water, while in the evening, paper lanterns were sent floating down the river.

Ornamentation of Ships

The spirit of the times manifested its pride in the magnificent deep-water ships of the period in a baroque abundance of decoration and ornament, in the designing and making of which artists and artisans joined hands. There must have been carvers of ships' ornaments in every European port of any significance. We know the fruits of their labors not only from paintings, graphics and ship models, from the collections of sculptured figureheads preserved in the marine museums of Paris, London, Karlskrona and Hamburg-Altona, but especially from the salvaging of the ship "Vasa" which capsized on her maiden voyage in Stockholm harbor in 1628. It will never be known just how it happened that this impressive three-master 66 meters long went to the bottom in a squall in sight of the shipyard after an all too brief career of one nautical mile. Following a long period of oblivion, the engineer Anders Franzén succeeded in 1956 in pinpointing the site of the wreck. The complicated operations necessary to salvage the wreck from a depth of 30 meters required extraordinary precautions and took from 1959 to 1961. The frigate proved to be an inexhaustible treasure of information, embodying the very peak of the multiform inventions of baroque ship decoration.

Carved, forged and painted decoration was used in the same parts of ships' hulls and rigging which have been favored ever since the times of the ancients: cutwater, stern, the mast trucks. Gun ports, bulwarks, quarter galleries and the interiors of cabins were also richly decorated. In the after sections of the ship the full wealth of brightly painted and lavishly gilded figurative and arabesque ornamentation was concentrated, wreathing about the ship's name and coat of arms of the home country or city (ill.84).

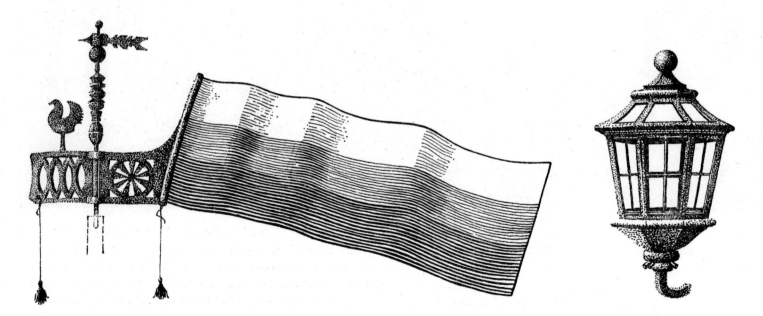

81 *The popular small vessels of the European coasting trades and fisheries were embellished with manifold decorations in painted, carved and forged work, displayed in the same parts of the ship as had been accentuated since the earliest times. Our examples show a carved wind vane from the White Sea and an artistically worked stern lantern from England (after Leonard Geoffrey Carr Laughton and A. A. Bobrinsky).*

82 Pieter Breughel the Elder (1528(?)–1569): Three-master and Galley. Next to the miniatures of the brothers van Eyck, the ship picture etchings of the Flemish Master W and some few paintings and graphic works by Hieronymus Bosch and Hans Holbein, Pieter Breughel the Elder's eleven engravings of different types of seagoing vessels, executed around 1564–1565, may be regarded as forerunners of marine painting.

Left:

*83 Dutch and French marine paint-
ing reached its perfection in the 17th
century. Willem van de Velde the
Younger (1633 to 1707) is regarded
as the principal representative of this
genre. His painting "Frigate in a Gale"
is in the Amsterdam Rijksmuseum.*

*84 Pride in the ships of world-wide
voyages found adequate expression in
the baroque profusion of ornamentation and decorated working parts of
vessels, in the production of which
artists and craftsmen united. At the
time, every European seaport of any
importance had marine carver's
workshops. The extent, style and
quality of their work can be studied in
the wreck find of the Swedish frigate
"Vasa", which foundered in 1628
and was salvaged in 1959–61. Our
picture shows the gilded carved lion
from the state coat of arms on the
transom of the ship.*

85 *Snobbish interest in navigation combined with the exaggerated hair styles of the ladies of the Court were responsible for this hairdress "à la Belle Poule", 1778, during the French rococo period of the 18th century. "La Belle Poule" was a well-known frigate of the French Navy.*

86 Whaling scene, painting on a wooden tea tray from Zaandam, Holland, 1772. In view of the great national importance of the arctic whale fisheries in the Netherlands during the 18th century, it was natural that artists should make use of the subjects offered by whaling and sealing in the execution of ornamentation on domestic utensils for the households of ships' captains and officers.

87 *Italian harbor scene, marine painting in the cover of a square piano built at Sonthofen, Allgäu (Bavaria), from the second half of the 18th century.*

88 Caspar David Friedrich (1774–1840): Sailing ship. Oil painting from about 1810.
The work of this German romantic artist, a native of Greifswald, contains many paintings and graphic compositions of sea and harbor scenes.

During the Renaissance the preferred stem decoration, the figurehead, was the lion, perhaps following herein the Venetians who were then leading in marine matters and whose vessels very commonly showed the lion of San Marco at the bow. During the Baroque other subjects made their appearance, e.g. mythological figures, such as Neptune and Triton with Naiads, Nereids and nixies.

The custom of decorating small vessels is also ancient and doubtless forms a regular part of folk art. Since the baroque period, however, sailors began to imitate the patrician and feudalist ways of the deep-water ships, especially in the Netherlands, in both the choice of motifs and technique of execution, and in multiplying the various section of a vessel that were to be ornamented. The bows of river and coastal boats were given carved nameboards and painted hawseholes. Carved and painted work was to be seen on mast steps, cabin doors and hatchways. In the after parts were artistically wrought stern lanterns and sockets for flagstaffs. The rudder head was adorned with a couchant lion or dolphin. At the truck, a carved wind vane rotated

(ill.81,90). Other boats might carry only the sign of the cross at the truck. Even the windowpanes of cabins were leaded with colored inserts. The Dutch coasters of our time, the tjalks, kuffs, botters and aaks, are still recognizable by their tasteful color schemes embellishing all parts of the vessel.

In baroque times the European ship décor was imitated by Arabs and Indians for their large deep-water merchantmen, the sterns of which were ornamented with motifs not native to these cultures. A baroque exuberance of embellishment comparable to the State vessels of European monarchs is displayed by the ceremonial barks of the rulers of Burma, Laos and Thailand (ill.80). Such vessels of pomp, with their gilt heads of snakes and swans, are still used today in Bangkok and Vientiane for the Buddhist ceremonial parades on feast days on the Menam and Mekong.

Left: 89 In Venice, antique and Christian traditions were intertwined in an impressive ceremonial: the Nuptials of the Doge with the Sea. Annually on Ascension Day the Head of the Republic was rowed in the galley "Bucintoro" —the model of which, in the Museo Storico Navale at Venice, is shown here—out into the Adriatic Sea. The state vessel was lavishly covered with gilt carvings and draped with crimson velvet. Its figurehead was the golden lion of San Marco. At sea, the Doge cast overboard a ring bearing the emblem of the Apostle St. Peter—boat and net—pronouncing the words: "I marry thee, oh Ocean, as a symbol of everlasting rule!"

90 Adorned rudder head in the shape of a lion from the Netherlands (after Tj. W. R. de Haan).

Clippers

At the beginning of the industrial revolution towards the end of the 18th century, when the first steam engines were being built, the typical ship for transoceanic voyages was the East Indiaman. These vessels were substantial three-masters of 40 to 50 meters overall length, carrying up to approximately 1500 tons deadweight; flax sails were just beginning to be used, instead of hempen ones, and their underwater bodies were protected by copper sheathing for retarding tropical marine growth. On the aftermost or mizzen mast, a square-headed gaff sail instead of the obsolete lateen sail was carried. Their rudders were controlled by steering wheels.

Today, half a dozen vessels closely akin to this type still exist, doing duty as ship museums: foremost, the "Victory", built in 1759–1765, once the flagship of Admiral Nelson, now preserved at Portsmouth in a drydock. The two American frigates "Constitution" and "Constellation", stationed at Boston and Baltimore respectively, likewise date back to the 18th century.

About the period mentioned, there began in the United States a development which in the 1830s was to revolutionize deep-water ship construction and was responsible for the ultimate flowering of worldwide navigation. We are speaking of the clippers. Several proven types of fast-sailing craft were the ancestors of the clippers: the sharp-built sloops of Bermudan and Jamaican waters, the luggers or *lougres* of Brittany, in which many Frenchmen had participated in the American War of Independence, also the fast schooners of Baltimore and Gloucester, which were renowned for quick cargo or fishing passages and had been successful both as smugglers and privateers. Features of these types were incorporated in the clippers, to begin with, at the time when fast-sailing vessels were wanted in the United States for smuggling opium from India to China.

The origin of the term "clipper" is controversial; whether it is derived from the verb, to clip; whether it must be traced back to the slang word "clipper" which means "a first-rate person or thing", has not been settled. But the identifying signs of the clipper ship are unmistakeable. They are vessels with a high, rising bow, pronounced sheer, overhangs fore and aft; long and narrow hulls, of a beam-to-length ratio of 1 : 5, previously unheard of. The masts were enormous, up to three-quarters of the length of the vessel. Other equally important characteristics were concave waterlines at the ships' ends, permitting a wedge-like splitting of the waves forward, and an easy, flowing detachment of the turbulent water aft. These are the features which all the capital windjammers combined, whose names were once familiar to all sailormen: "Rainbow", "Oriental", "Westward-Ho", "Great Republic", "Sovereign of the Seas", "Flying Cloud"—all of American build; and the English "Ariel", "Cutty Sark" and countless others.

Let us stress the fact that the clippers did not originate on the drawing boards of engineers, but were created by craftsmen, although with such care and knowledge as to raise them to the level of artists. First a log was roughly dimensioned and shaped to the scale of the proposed hull, then the refinements were gradually added. When at last the lines corresponded in all aspects to the combined ideas of commissioner and builder the latter would saw his model into a dozen or so transverse slabs. Each slab was then enlarged on the floor of the mould loft, to correspond to the actual dimensions and serve as a model for a rib mould. The moulds were used to select the most suited, naturally bent oak timbers from the carefully hoarded supplies in the timber yard, and according to these moulds the shipwrights shaped the ribs of the vessel.

91 *The fast and astonishingly consistent passages of the American clippers from east coast ports around Cape Horn to the gold country of California became very quickly advertised in the widely distributed handbills and posters of the various shipping lines.*

These were the times, both in Europe and the United States, of the first dawn of the science of shipbuilding technology, the age of the first vocational trade schools teaching courses in naval design, the first handbooks of technical drafting and calculations. The most prominent builder of clipper ships, Donald McKay, who worked in Boston from 1843 until 1880, was rightly regarded in the United States as an artist of national rank. Although his shipyard had steam-driven saws and wood-turning lathes, he continued to shape his models from his own craftsman-like experience, relying chiefly on his eye and hand. McKay fitted his ships with the latest American inventions, which materially eased the labors of working the vessel: wire pendents for braces and wherever else possible, ball-bearing patent blocks and patent winches with geared cogwheel transmissions.

The history of the clippers is indissolubly connected with some typically capitalist enterprises: the opium smuggling trade of the thirties and forties of the 19th century; the gold rush to California which began in 1848 and which made the doubling of dangerous Cape Horn a routine matter, furnishing a theme for American advertising techniques (ill.91); lastly, the intrusion of American ship owners in the tea trade from China to London after repeal of the British Navigation Laws, which previously had protected her domestic shipping interests. In 1850 the first American clipper to win the "tea race" docked in the Thames; the passage from Hongkong to England had taken 97 days. The freight earned by this record trip paid for three-quarters of the building cost of the vessel.

92 Baltimore clipper
(after Sam Svensson & Gordon Macfie).

93 Lithographs of gripping scenes of clipper sailing—such as the finish of the Tea Race between "Ariel" and "Taeping" in 1866, became in the 1850s and 1860s some of the main features of illustrated newspapers and magazines in Great Britain and the U.S.A. Produced in large editions and widely distributed, they also became popular as domestic decorations. To this day one of these prints occasionally turns up in some remote place on the European coast, whence they had been brought by sailors returning home, who had bought them in the souvenir stores of Liverpool, London, Antwerp or Hamburg.

94 *Antoine Roux (1765–1835) of Marseilles was a prominent marine painter, whose work we are illustrating with the watercolor of a xebec, a vessel rigged with three lateen sails and native to Spain, North Africa and the Levant. Xebecs and feluccas were the archetypal elegant, fast Mediterranean craft.*

95 Eduard Hildebrandt (1818–1869): Chinese Junk. Watercolor, 1863. This artist, a native of Danzig (Gdánsk) who later lived in Berlin, may be considered to be the most important German marine painter of the 19th century. From 1862 to 1864 he went on a journey around the world, from which he brought home magnificent studies of vessels from Far Eastern waters.

96 Figurehead of the bark "Pommern", built 1903 at Glasgow, now forming part of the Ålands Sjöfartsmuseum as museum ship. With her four tall masts visible from afar, she has become a symbol of the Finnish island town of Mariehamn.

97 Bow of the clipper ship "Cutty Sark", at Greenwich, London. This full-rigged ship, built in England in 1869, whose name refers to the "scanty shift" of the witch Nanny in the poem by the Scottish poet Burns, was a famous racer and often logged as much as 17 knots. After several decades of voyages in the tea and wool trade to China and Australia, the vessel was used as a stationary school ship after 1922. Since 1957 "Cutty Sark" has been in a dry dock and is now a restored museum ship.

134

98 From the end of the 19th
century on, every seaport of
any significance had at least
one "harbor photographer",
who photographed not only
the local ships, but any remarkable vessel touching there,
selling the prints to crews,
their relatives, and to ship
lovers in general. Today the
collections of negatives
of the harbor photographers
form a valuable part of the
archives of many marine
museums. We show here a
rare photograph of the only
five-masted full-rigged ship
ever built, the "Preussen",
built in 1902 at Geestemünde.
This steel ship belonged to
the Hamburg sailing ship
firm of F. Laeisz.
She could load 8000 tons of
bulk cargo. In 1910, on her
14th voyage, the "Preussen"
was lost in the English
Channel after a collision.

Right:
99 Japan is one of those
seafaring nations that still
attach importance to training
under sail. The Institute of
Sea Training owns two
sailing training ships. One
of these is the four-masted
bark "Nippon Maru", built
in 1930 and illustrated here.
Officer candidates for the
merchant marine serve in
these vessels for one year on
long voyages, after three
years at navigation school.
They complete their training
in a modern motor ship.

*100 The six-masted fore-and-aft schooner "Wyoming" built at Bath,
Maine, on the east coast of the U.S.A. in 1907. The overall length
of 108 meters made this the longest wooden sailing-ship ever built.*

The Last of the Large Sailing Merchantmen

Her Majesty's Admiralty begged permission of the skipper of the "Oriental", which had become famous overnight, to measure and take off the lines of the clipper in drydock.

Clipper sailing stands for high daily averages under varying conditions of wind direction and strength; in a few instances, 250 miles a day have been reached or even exceeded; it stands for rounding Cape Horn under topgallant sails when other ships would be carrying reefed topsails. Much has been written on the theme of the clippers. The best contributions to the topic are still Howard Chapelle's "History of American Sailing Ships" and Basil Lubbock's series of works dealing with the opium, tea and colonial clippers. About the middle forties of the last century a special literary genre arose in the U.S. and a little later, in Europe: the sea novel, the authors of which have frequently experienced sea life—Herman Melville, Jack London, Pierre Loti, Joseph Conrad, to name a few.

From the 1850s on, and especially after iron became the building material, the lengths of ships increased to exceed the 100-meter limit, at a beam-to-length ratio of approximately 1 : 7.5. The necessary differentiation of the towering sail area of such giants was achieved through dividing the topsails and, not much later, the topgallant sails also. A last version of the wooden-hulled merchant sailing ship was the composite build, which combined iron ribs and longitudinal bracing with wood planking. One of the fastest representatives of the type, the "Cutty Sark", built in 1869, is still intact as a ship museum in London (ill.97). After Siemens' adaptation of the Martin method of cast steel production for industrial uses in the 1870s, shipyards soon began to replace iron with steel for large sailing vessels, which then began to be rigged as four-masters, first as full-riggers, later on almost exclusively as barks. In England an excellent compromise between clipper lines and profitable cargo carrying qualities had developed since the early part of the last century,

101 Four-masted bark.

"...The ivory Pequod was turned into what seemed a shamble; every sailor a butcher. ... In the first place, the enormous cutting tackles, among other ponderous things comprising a cluster of blocks generally painted green, and which no single man can possibly lift—this vast bunch of grapes was swayed up to the main-top and firmly lashed to the lower masthead ... The end of the hawser-like rope winding through these intricacies, was then conducted to the windlass, and the huge lower block of the tackles was swung over the whale; to this block the great blubber hook, weighing some one hundred pounds, was attached. And now suspended in stages over the side, Starbuck and Stubb, the mates, armed with their long spades, began cutting a hole in the body for the insertion of the hook just above the nearest of the two side-fins. This done, a broad, semicircular line is cut round the hole, the hook is inserted, and the main body of the crew striking up a wild chorus, now commence heaving in one dense crowd at the windlass. When instantly, the entire ship careens over on her side; every bolt in her starts like the nailheads of an old house in frosty weather; she trembles, quivers, and nods her frightened mastheads to the sky. More and more she leans over the whale, while every gasping heave of the windlass is answered by a helping heave from the billows; till at last, a swift, startling snap is heard; with a great swash the ship rolls upwards and backwards from the whale, and the triumphant tackle rises into sight, dragging after it the disengaged semicircular end of the first strip of blubber..."

"Besides her hoisted boats, an American whaler is outwardly distinguished by her try-works. ... It is as if from the open field a brick-kiln were transported to her planks. The try-works are planted between the foremast and mainmast, the most roomy part of the deck. The timbers beneath are of a peculiar strength, fitted to sustain the weight of an almost solid mass of brick and mortar, some ten feet by eight square, and five in height. ... On the flanks it is cased with wood, and at top completely covered by a large, sloping, battened hatchway. Removing this hatch we expose the great try-pots, two in number, and each of several barrels' capacity. ... Removing the fire-board from the front of the try-works, the bare masonry of that side is exposed, penetrated by the two iron mouths of the furnaces, directly beneath the pots. These mouths are fitted with heavy doors of iron. The intense heat of the fire is prevented from communicating itself to the deck, by means of a shallow reservoir extending under the entire inclosed surface of the works. By a tunnel inserted at the rear, this reservoir is kept replenished with water as fast as it evaporates. There are no external chimneys; they open direct from the rear wall."

Herman Melville:
Moby Dick,
1851

102 North American whaler (after Sam Svensson & Gordon Macfie).

in the "Blackwall frigates" built near London, a type which outlasted the clippers and became a model for the last windjammers in the wool, grain and nitrate trades. In 1881 the final phase of dimensional increase set in, when American yards built the first five-masted fore-and-aft schooners. In 1890 the French shipowner Bordes risked the building of a first five-masted square-rigger. The few other five-masted steel monsters which followed the lead of "France", e.g. the "Preussen", 135 meters long, of the Hamburg firm of Laeisz, could load up to 8000 tons of bulk cargo. Nearly all of them were employed in the nitrate trade with Chile (ill. 98).

We must not allow our enthusiasm for this magnificent final chapter of deep-water sailing ship lore to make us forget that there were then, besides the huge windjammers, a great many other, smaller sailing craft, whose sailors accomplished just as much. Not to speak of fishing and coastal vessels, we will remind readers only of the whaling ships of the American New England states. Herman Melville has erected a lasting literary monument to their sailors in his "Moby Dick".

103 View of the stern of the museum ship "Cutty Sark".

Right:
Chinese caricature of a sidewheeler, about 1850 (after Chr. Lloyd & J. Donglas-Henry).

Some Developments in Powered Ships

1802 in England	Successful trial trip of Symington's sidewheel tug "Charlotte Dundas" with a Watt 10 hp engine.
1807 in the U.S.A.	Fulton introduces regular trips on the Hudson River with the sidewheeler "Clermont".
1819 in the U.S.A.	The frigate "Savannah" crosses the North Atlantic, fitted with an effective auxiliary steam engine of 90 hp.
1822 in England	Completion of the first iron steam ship "Aaron Manby".
1829 in Trieste	Ressel's screw steamer "Civetta" abandons her trial trip after a few minutes on account of breakage of a steam pipe. Later on, Smith in England and Ericsson in the U.S.A. succeeded in the technical perfection of screw propellers.
1838 in England	Up to this time, the prevalent ship engines were the modified Watt type, in which power was transmitted indirectly from the piston crosshead to the crank actuating the wheels by way of a lateral beam. John Penn's direct-action engine with "oscillating" swinging cylinders (ill. 111) proves to be the most efficient low-pressure motive power for ships.
1847 in Scotland	Caird of Greenock builds the first inverted engines for steamers, in which the cylinders are situated above the crankshaft.
1858 in Scotland	John Elder combines the double-expansion inverted engine with a surface condenser. With "compound engines" of this type steam navigation begins to be profitable: coal consumption is reduced by one half, compared with the simple low-pressure type of engine.
1881 in England	The Cunard express steamer "Servia" is the first seagoing ship to be fitted with electric lighting.
1882 in Scotland	Kirk fits out the "Aberdeen" with the first triple-expansion inverted engine (with steel boiler) working at a pressure of 9 atmospheres absolute pressure.
1897 in England	Parsons' experimental turbine vessel "Turbinia" opens a new era in seagoing thermal expansion engines. A climax is reached in 1908 with the record trip of the Cunard giant "Mauretania", with her 68,000 hp turbines.
1959 in the U.S.S.R.	The icebreaker "Lenin" successfully completes her trial run as the first merchant vessel with nuclear reactor steam turbines.

The introduction of steam power brought about an essential change in sea life. Previously sailors alone had worked the vessel jointly with their captain and mates, who had risen to their rank through learning the necessary navigational skills. From Symington and Fulton on, the "black gang" entered the scene; all those who, below decks, stoked the boilers, trimmed coal and operated the valves (ill.107). On the maiden run of a new steamer they were at first landlubbers, strangers from another world of boilermakers and plumbers, iron works and engineering shops. Granted that they might speak the same dialect of the coast as their comrades on deck: they were outsiders for all that, bringing the smell of coal and hot grease into the forecastle; one saw them in a flickering, demoniac light, in the glow of fires, wreathed about by wisps of steam.

From the early 19th century on, something like a "third estate" evolved among seamen, possessed of their own community symbols and their own technical jargon. This is illustrated, for instance, in the skin-pricked devices of tattooing. The deck crew went in for anchors, flags, sailing ships. The "black gang" had quite different professional symbols: trimmer's slices and pokers, firemen's shovels, steam and water gauge, hammer and wrench (ill.104).

It was the engine room personnel, stokers and trimmers, who gave the first impulse for the trade union organization of maritime workers: first in England and, after 1890, following repeal of the Socialist Law, also in Germany. In 1897 the seagoing proletariat united in the "International Federation of Ship and Dock Workers".

With steam navigation the superiority of Europeans and North Americans in worldwide sea trade became indisputable. From here on we encounter the attitude of patronizing contempt for the navigational achievements of non-industrialized peoples, who are dismissed as "primitives". We may note in passing that the standing of the English language as the international sailors' idiom has been confirmed only since the time of the industrial revolution. Earlier, in northern European sea life, Dutch had been dominant, and not merely in a linguistic sense: bourgeois Holland had been a cultural model for long periods, while other parts of the world had oriented themselves to the Portuguese and Spanish languages.

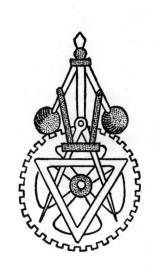

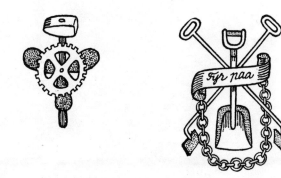

104 The tattoos of engine-room personnel — emblems of their working tools as professional insignia — reflect the interests of this social group. Our illustration is taken from the sample book of the Copenhagen tattooing artist Niels Fischer. The book is now in the Danish Marine Museum at Castle Kronborg.

Steam Navigation in Art

There are relatively few instances of the appearance of steamships in the plastic arts. The French ship painter Antoine Roux seems to have been much impressed by them. He has painted many of the early yachtlike side-wheelers which in his times entered the port of Marseilles. More recently two expressionists, Lyonel Feininger and Emil Nolde, have demonstrated the special charm to be found in tugboats and other small steamers (ill.105,106). There are comparatively few representations of steamers among the ship portraits of the 19th century. This fact finds its explanation in the ownership situation: for the master of a sailing-ship, the portrait of his command was a status symbol, but the generality of steamers were not owned by individual captains, but by capitalist shipping firms or lines. Much more frequent than painted steamer portraits are lithographs of steamers, often in conjunction with views of towns. There was hardly a place on the coast which omitted to have "its" steamer portrayed, after the system of regularly scheduled steamboat connections was established, ornamenting the timetable with the illustration. The old-time harbor photographers also took much pleasure in the silhouettes and smoketrails of steamers.

105 Emil Nolde (1867–1956):
Fishing vessel. Woodcut, 1910.
From: Gustav Schiefler,
Das graphische Werk von Emil Nolde
1910–1925, 1927.

106 Lyonel Feininger (1871–1956):
Sidewheeler II. Oil painting, 1913.

The expressionist painters Emil Nolde and Lyonel Feininger
discovered almost at the same time the artistic interest offered by
steamers, especially the smaller types. Feininger began to paint in
1907. His earlier work in the cubist manner is based on nature
sketches made during the summer, many of them in the region around
Rügen and Usedom. The composition may have been inspired by the
resort steamers running between these islands in those days.

Left:

107 Firing up the ship's furnace. During the period of coal-burning boilers, the labors of firemen and trimmers were the hardest and the worst paid on board. Furnace room work in the giant express steamers of the big North Atlantic passenger lines during the crossing of the ocean—described in the prospectus for passenger consumption as a "bus ride to New York"—commonly resembled the worst slave labor. Technically, the construction of marine piston steam engines reached a climax in these liners. The most powerful plant was that of the "Deutschland", built in 1900 at Stettin (Szczecin): two six-cylinder quadruple-expansion engines each yielding 17,800 hp. Thirty-two furnaces produced in the 16 boilers an operating pressure of 15 atmospheres absolute pressure. The total effect of almost 36,000 hp activated twin screws of a diameter of 7 meters.

108 Steamship owner Börgesson of Karlskrona. Caricature, around 1900. The Swedish local newspaper from which the cartoon is taken, was ridiculing one of those small shipowners typical, before the First World War, of local steamer traffic in most European countries. Entrepreneurs of his kind very often ran but a single vessel, doing duty as occasion demanded, as ferry, tugboat, beach tripper or Sunday afternoon excursion steamer. During the week, Börgesson was a machinist in the Royal Navy Yard. On weekends he operated a passenger service between the harbor town and the countless rocky islets of the vicinity.

109 This tin toy steamer "Excelsior", of the middle of the 19th century, is viewed by many scholars of the history of mechanical toys as a specimen of an indigenous North American product, not fashioned in any way after a European prototype. Steam navigation on the Mississippi–Missouri waterways began as early as 1812. There was a time when the river steamers were more popular than the railroads. Between 90 and 120 meters long, they had room for some 2000 passengers; speeds of up to 23 knots were attained. Each of the two single-cylinder, low-pressure engines transmitted the upward thrust of the vertical piston by way of a connecting rod and beam indirectly to one of the big bucket-wheels. Mark Twain has created a literary monument to this kind of vessel. Two picturesque veterans have been preserved as museums in the United States: "W. P. Snyder" and "Ticonderoga"; the latter was a lake steamer in New England and is now exhibited on land in Vermont. The "Delta Queen" of Cincinnati is still active in the tourist service; one of her main attractions is her calliope, a steam organ with 32 pipes, on the uppermost deck.

110 Steamer model of the middle of the 19th century. From 1816 on steamboats navigated on the Rhine as far as Cologne. Replicas of these vehicles were used as props on the stage of the "Köllschen Faxenmacher" (a team of music-hall entertainers) for their rod-puppet comedies with the local characters Tünnes, Schääl and Hännes.

111 Oscillating steam engine of the sidewheel steamer "Hjeilen", built 1861 in the Jutland town of Silkeborg, west of Århus. The oldest iron steamship still in commission in the world, she is a great tourist attraction. "Hjeilen" still steams along with the engine installed more than a century ago: a two-cylinder plant yielding 25 hp and revolving at 35 rpm. In oscillating steam engines the cylinders are situated below the crank shaft. The piston thrust is upward and acts directly on the shaft axle crank without connecting rod. Seated in oscillating trunnions, the cylinders follow the rotary motion of the crank. Compared to the indirect action of the Watt type of reciprocating engine, the rotary type taking effect directly on the shaft was, in the evolution of steam marine power, a first step toward sensible economy both in weight and in space.

112 *The North American four-masted fore-and-aft schooner*
"Cordelia E. Hayes" ready for launching; Bath, Maine, U.S.A.
In the career of a ship, beginning and end are traditionally distin-
guished by various customs. Life begins, upon completion of building,
with the naming ceremony, the christening. In all epochs and all
over the world it was and is customary to combine the conclusion of
construction, the naming of the vessel in some hallowing ritual, and
the launching into an impressive celebration. James Hornell and
Bronislaw Malinowski have described the folk customs attending ship-
hallowing in India and Oceania. There, the festivities were prepared
by choosing certain days and hours that were believed to be lucky; the
ceremonies began by decorating the raft or boat with colored cloths,
strings of beads, flower garlands and wreaths. Ornamental designs
were painted on the sides of the vessel with colored paste; incense was
burned, and the vessel was illuminated with oil lamps. Sacrificial

offerings were deposited at the bow, accompanied by gesturing, song
and dances. Such gifts consisted in India, for example, of coconuts
split in half, rice tarts and a goblet filled with rice brandy. A goblet
was passed from father to son in seafaring families through many
generations, reserved for this ritual purpose. A ceremonial dousing
with water and the proclamation of the name in flowery speech an-
nounced the climax of the feast: the sacrifice of a chicken or sheep, its
blood anointing the prow of the new vessel. In other parts of the
country a pumpkin scored into segments and filled with some red
coloring matter was fastened to the cutwater; when the vessel was
launched, the pumpkin burst and spilled its contents over the bows.
The male youths escorted the christened and hallowed vessel to its
element with singing, hallooing and fireworks; the day was ended with
festive banqueting, a procession, playing and dancing. Elements of
archaic customs continue to mark launching ceremonies in industrial-

ized shipyards in contemporary Japan: at the bow of a modern ship, decorated with flowers and draped in bunting, a large paper sphere is fitted, composed of loosely joined red and white segments; it is filled with balloons, paper snakes and confetti, and just prior to the launching, live pigeons are put inside. As the ship glides down the ways the sphere bursts, its colorful contents showering the guests; the pigeons and balloons, harbingers of good luck, flutter and float off into space. As was the beginning, the end of a vessel is often attended by some tradition. No true sailor will demolish his wrecked vessel, unless compelled by authority or necessity. Remnants of this sentiment can be observed everywhere. The countless "ships' graveyards" in or near harbors the world over, are often not just the outcome of insufficient regard for tidiness, but a last echo of maritime folk tradition. In New Guinea the big community boats used to be given regular burials, and the tools with which the vessel had been built were put in the grave as funerary gifts.

113 In this semi-industrialized boatyard in southern Norway, series of wooden and fiberglass boats were built side by side (1966). Despite the new material and the new technology, the plastic hulls were shaped according to the traditional form of the clinker-built wooden boats.

114 Hot-bulb motor in a small fishing cutter from the Oderhaff. A hot-bulb motor is an internal combustion engine using crude oil; the fuel is exploded at approximately 15 atmospheres absolute pressure by means of surface ignition at the red hot-bulb on the cylinder head. The older four-cycle engines were structurally modelled after inverted vertical steam engines; the water-cooled cylinder of these massive, slow-rotation plants was placed on columns above the exposed crank-shaft. In 1902 Eric Rundlöf of Stockholm constructed the two-stroke hot-bulb motor with enclosed crankshaft. One of the last hot-bulb motors on the coast of the German Baltic, a 20 hp Bolinder model, is in operation in the small cutter of Danish build — whence its name "De lütt Dän" (little Dane) —which was used by the Berliner Akademie-Institut für Deutsche Volkskunde for its maritime-ethnographical research from 1958 to 1969.

"When he stepped aboard a big fine steamboat, he entered a new and marvelous world: chimney-tops cut to counterfeit a spraying crown of plumes—and maybe painted red; pilot-house, hurricane-deck, boiler-deck guards, all garnished with white wooden filigree-work of fanciful patterns; gilt acorns topping the derricks; gilt deer horns over the big bell; gaudy symbolical picture painted on the paddle-box, possibly; big roomy boiler-deck, painted blue, and furnished with Windsor arm-chairs; inside, a far-receding snow-white "cabin"; porcelain knob and oil-picture on every stateroom door; curving patterns of filigree-work touched up with gilding, stretching overhead all down the converging vista; big chandeliers every little way, each an April shower of glittering glass drops. ...in the ladies' cabin a pink and white Wilton carpet, as soft as mush, and glorified with a ravishing pattern of gigantic flowers. Then the Bridal Chamber ... whose pretentious flummery was necessarily overawing to the now tottering intellect of the hosannahing citizen. ... Take the steamboat which I have just described, and you have her in her highest and finest, and most pleasing, and comfortable, and satisfactory estate. Now cake her over with a layer of ancient and obdurate dirt, and you have the Cincinnati steamer awhile ago referred to."

Mark Twain:
Life on the Mississippi,
1883

"... and the whole lofty space resembled the interior of a monument, divided by floors of iron grating, with lights flickering at different levels, and a mass of gloom lingering in the middle, within the columnar stir of machinery under the motionless swelling of the cylinders.

A loud and wild resonance, made up of all the noises of the hurricane, dwelt in the still warmth of the air. There was in it the smell of hot metal, of oil, and a slight mist of steam. The blows of the sea seemed to traverse it in an unringing, stunning shock, from side to side.

Gleams, like pale long flames, trembled upon the polish of metal; from the flooring below the enormous crank-heads emerged in their turns with a flash of brass and steel—going over; while the connecting rods, big-jointed, like skeleton limbs, seemed to thrust them down and pull them up again with an irresistible precision. And deep in the half-light other rods dodged deliberately to and fro, crossheads nodded, discs of metal rubbed smoothly against each other, slow and gentle, in a commingling of shadows and gleams. ...

The wood-encased bulk of the low-pressure cylinder, frowning portly from above, emitted a faint wheeze at every thrust, and except for that low hiss the engines worked their steel limbs headlong or slow with a silent, determined smoothness. And all this, the white walls, the moving steel, the floor plates under Solomon Rout's feet, the floors of iron grating above his head, the dusk and the gleams, uprose and sank continuously, with one accord, upon the harsh wash of the waves against the ship's side. The whole loftiness of the place, booming hollow to the great voice of the wind, swayed at the top like a tree, would go over bodily, as if borne down this way and that by the tremendous blasts."

Joseph Conrad:
Typhoon,
1903

In literature we do not find many steamers. While there are several dozen really good works dealing with shipboard life under canvas, few writers have found steam navigation worthy of their attention: Mark Twain, in his memories of the years when he was a river pilot on the Mississippi; Joseph Conrad, who had been a master mariner. Gerhart Hauptmann created in 1909, in his novel "Atlantis", concerning the tragic voyage of an imaginary express steamer "Roland", a visionary anticipation of the catastrophe of the "Titanic". Bernhard Traven is the author of the deeply moving epic of firemen and coal trimmers in his "Totenschiff" (Ship of the Dead).

On the other hand, folk art has not disdained the steamer. We count among its expressions the ballads of popular singers, recounting famous burnings and collisions of steamers. There are also countless jocular little ditties dealing with local situations, ridiculing small vessels in provincial traffic:

> "Here comes little Lykkeby,
>   Never rings his bell, not he—
> Going straight to Frauendorf,
> Comes right back with a load of turf."

Folk humor also created the plenitude of sometimes really loving, yet ridiculing, nicknames for these vessels: "Lame Duck" for "Dolphin", "Stiff in the Knee" for "Stephanie", or "Stockholm Witch", "Fire-eater", "Flounder", "Rattletrap", "Ditch Crawler", etc. The "Colerein", purchased from England, was maligned as the "Cholera", out of the "God with Us" the sailors made "God help Us".

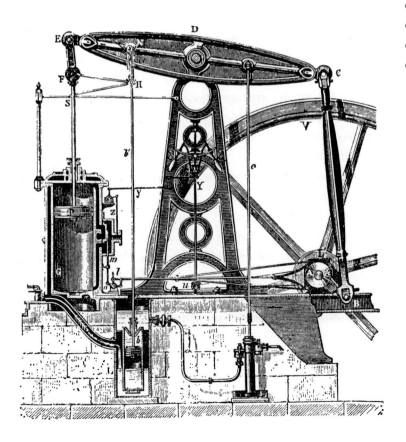

115 Oscillating steam engine by James Watt (after P. Appell & J. Chapius).

Sailors and Mechanization

Hot-bulb
or Surface Ignition Motors

In the early constructive phase of development of the innovations of hot-bulb and outboard motors, to be further discussed below, we perceive a last manifestation of pre-industrial, popular technique founded on personal experience and individual "puttering". Unlike conventional steam engines, turbines or diesels, their operation can be mastered by the ordinary sailor himself, without having to resort to specialized engine-room personnel, and this generated a new type of navigation in fisheries and coastwise trading, without further division of work responsibilities and skills.

The daily handling of motors by seamen necessarily led to a considerable enlargement of knowledge over the course of time. Through the 19th century, in the sheds of fishermen on the European waterways one would find only the ancient, inherited tools of woodworking: axe and saw, hammer and pliers, auger, wood chisel and knife, as well as the indispensable net-making needles of course. The only measuring devices known popularly were the footrule, yardstick and mesh-gauge board. After 1900 the picture changes. With motorization, the necessary tools had to be added: vice, wrenches, screwdriver, metal chisel and drills, thread cutter and soldering iron. The slide gauge likewise became indispensable. The hereditary knowledge of materials used in the work of fishermen and small-craft sailors—mostly natural products like wood, textiles or webs made of animal or vegetal matter, passed on from one generation to the next for centuries—underwent a gradual increase and broadening, covering materials, concepts and methods belonging to a different working world, the essential knowledge of mechanics based on metal. All these innovations were in the beginning communicated by the direct means of demonstration and imitation, but by and by the transfer of knowledge was raised to a higher level through the introduction of special training courses, handbooks, professional literature and vocational schools.

Motorized navigation of small vessels began with attempts to fit fishing craft with crude-oil engines. Priestman and Gardner in England, Swiderski in Germany, worked at the problem. The difficulty lay in assuring reliable functioning of the motors, necessitating a permanently burning heating lamp with the double function of heating the induction duct in the cylinder head as well as the carburetor. No practical solution had been found. No skipper, no matter how progressively minded, wanted to have to live with this kind of hazard, the more so as all early trials had been failures: in 1892, the Bremen fishing cutter "Matador", in Holland a lugger, in England in 1895 the fishing vessel "Lesly". A skipper of the North Friesian island of Amrum paid for incurring the perils of technical progress with the loss of his wooden schooner, set ablaze by careless handling of the fuel.

The Englishman Akroyd took out a patent for a crude-oil motor with self-ignition by means of highly compressed induction air in 1890. Shortly after this date, some Scandinavian master mechanics, experimenting independently from one another, materially improved this method through the inclusion of a cast-iron "hot bulb" screwed into the cylinder head, which had to be preheated with a blow torch just before starting the motor. When the bulb was red-hot, the injected crude-oil spray ignited in the stream of compressed air. Once the motor was started, the explosions maintained the required heat of the bulb. This solution worked well. Each succeeding year saw more surface ignition engines installed in Denmark and Sweden. Factory names like Alpha, Bolinder, Dan, Gideon and Skandia became household words among sailors almost overnight (ill. 114).

Bolinder, placing the two-stroke cycle engine of his designer Rundlöf on the market in Stockholm in 1903, definitely opened the road for motorization of fishing and coastwise vessels, and not only in northern Europe. Hot-bulb ignition engines were already running in the Adriatic Sea, in Indonesia, China, Japan and South America, while diesel engines for large ships existed only on the drawing boards of the designers. In 1911 the news that the schooner "Lingueta", fitted with a 30 hp Bolinder motor, had travelled 4500 nautical miles from London to Pernambuco under power alone, created a sensation. The engine had run like clockwork on the trip.

The first diesel-driven ships began to navigate in 1904 on the Volga and on the Lake of Geneva. They were, in Russia, the Nobel tankers "Vandal" and "Sarmat", in Switzerland the little "Venoga". The Dutch began operating the first seagoing diesel vessel when they launched the tanker "Vulcanus" in 1910, to be followed in 1912 by the Danish East India freighters "Selandia" and "Fionia". But only in the early 1930s was there any serious and broad use of diesel engines in small vessels, after the Deutz Works developed the pre-combustion chamber, combined with L'Orange's invention of wick ignition with saltpeter paper. In the fisheries and the coastwise trade of Scandinavia, Germany and the Netherlands, the hot-bulb motor ruled the field more or less without competition until the outbreak of the Second World War. About the heaviest versions of this type of engine were those in the powerful towboats of the Danube. In 1950 Bolinder discontinued the production of hot-bulb motors, but they are still to be found, however rarely, distributed from the Lofoten Islands to Newfoundland, and to Lake Chad in Central Africa.

Far beyond Europe the hot-bulb engine had motorized small craft navigation and, in Europe, the fishing fleets. Another type of engine was needed, however, to mechanize the hundreds of thousands of small fishing boats everywhere in the world: dugouts, kayaks, rafts, rowing boats and catamarans. Such hulls needed a power plant that could be quickly installed in the boat, easily started, and which did not require complex mechanical manipulations for either use or maintenance. Such motors had already existed since 1905 in two versions: one and two-cylinder types, which could be mounted either vertically at the stern or diagonally over the side of the boat, eggbeater fashion. Makers of these engines were Ole Evinrude in Milwaukee, U.S.A., and Fritz Ziegenspeck in Berlin, whose products were commercially known as "Effzett", which sounded better (ill. 116).

116 *Advertising for "Effzett" outboard motors in the Annual of 1911 of the German motor-boat club.*

Evinrude, a Norwegian by birth, had named his motor "outboard" because all parts of the engine were outside the boat's hull. The first clients for these lightweight power plants were water sportsmen on both sides of the Atlantic. Gasoline motors were already very popular in American waters, with a low first cost as well as convenient servicing because of American mass production methods. The professional fishermen of Canada, Alaska, Greenland, Labrador, Mexico and the Antilles, and of both coasts of South America, soon took advantage of the situation. Before long, outboard motors made by Evinrude, Johnson, Chrysler or Mercury, could be seen driving Caribbean dugouts as well as kayaks of the Eskimos and Jangada rafts in Brazil. Standard replacement parts were available even in the primeval forests of the Amazon and in the islands of Tierra del Fuego. At the end of the Second World War there was a vast increase of production, when portions of the U.S. automobile and airplane industries re-tooled their systems for boat motor making. This flood of series numbering hundreds of thousands after 1955, completed the motorization of fishing boats in the remotest corners of the globe.

At the turn of the century the boatbuilding industry in northern Europe was experimenting with the fabrication of small boats in new materials: first in metal, then, from 1952 on, based on models coming from the U.S.A., in fiberglass. At the initial stage of this development the search for solutions to formal problems is of some interest to the historian. In Norway, for example, the side-by-side building of wooden planked boats and boats of plastic construction could be observed in boatyards operating on a semi-industrialized basis (ill. 113). The builder conditioned by the handicraft tradition "thought wood" and acted accordingly: he gave the vessel to be produced not at all the kind of structure the new material would have suggested, but copied the old wooden planked boat as it had evolved through so many generations. A similar tendency had previously occurred before the First World War in the Netherlands and elsewhere, where the local craftsmen shifted to iron construction, but continued to reproduce the traditional lines of the wooden types (tjalk, schooner, galleas, etc.). They even went so far as to copy in iron traditional details of the wooden boats, which hybrid vessels were aptly called "mules" or "jackasses" by skippers.

Right:
Max Pechstein (1881–1955): Return from the fishing grounds (Rowe).
Pen drawing, 1930.
From: Max Pechstein, Erinnerungen, 1960

Life in the World of Sailors and Fishermen

Partnership Crews

It is a curious fact that not only most ship enthusiasts, but even a majority of modern nautical experts connect the idea of a command structure with their concept of social relations amongst the men aboard a ship, i.e. a situation wherein a commander at the top issues orders executed by those under him. However, this kind of crew relationship represents neither the original social structure, nor is it even applicable now without reservations, at least not in small craft navigation and in fishing vessels.

During the period of early Carolingian feudalism of the 8th century, we find a first mention of maritime confederation in Flanders, the *conjurationes* of those who go to sea. In 1097 the crews of similarly manned ships of Flanders and Friesland were designated as *consodales*, i.e. partners. Not much later, the *Rôles d'Oléron*, probably dating from the 12th century, which originated in the coastal area of the Franco-Basque Atlantic countries and constitute the oldest codified North European maritime law, state unmistakably that in those days a partnership type of crew did exist, resembling social conditions still found today in the Scandinavian countries, on the southern Baltic coast and on the Friesian North Sea coast, and which certainly existed elsewhere at one time or another. The social patterning of ships' crews, stemming from the partnership fashion of thinking and acting which developed during the latter phases of primeval society, remained virtually unchanged through many centuries. As recently as the first half of the 20th century, it not only governed shoreside fishing in broad regions of northern Europe, but was also fully operative in coastwise cargo navigation, especially in Scandinavia.

The characteristic feature of a partnership crew was the equality of the position of crew members in the work to be done on board. This equality was often based on joint ownership of the vessel, which might be divided either in equal parts or apportioned shares. The decisive factor was not the amount of property invested in the ship, but the nature of the division of labor on a basis of a commonalty of rights, whether in rowing or making sail, steering or, in more recent times, running the ship's engine. During stretches of continuous hard work—rowing, steering, tacking ship, lowering or hoisting in of the fishing gear, manning the pump, etc.—there was often a periodic alternation of the work stations, based on experience and standardized by local tradition. Other important duties, for instance cooking, were rotated at longer intervals, perhaps every week. Fixed job assignments did not exist. In consequence of this, professional titles indicative of rank or position were completely absent in the partnership crew: a skipper was unknown in such vessels. Where some shore authority insisted on the crew designating a responsible member, the decision might be made along some such lines as the following, which comes from Sweden: "Olaf, you put your name down—you know how to read and write!" An "official" machinist might be nominated on the strength of the chosen individual being the bearer of the matchbox, with which to light the blow torch for warming up the hot bulb. Ancient traditions are preserved in the terms used in Low German to designate the members of a ship's company: *Maschop, Maat, Macker* and *Kump*. A work group composed of such men was called in Sweden *båtlag*; in Germany, *Partie, Kommüne, Matschopei* or *Kumpschaft*.

*117 Indian fishing boat crew
of the coast of Kerala.*

*118 A "fleece" at the stem of a Portuguese fishing boat from the
province of Algarve. The carving is intended to resemble a bunched
lambskin. Very recently this stem ornament, which is still common
in Mediterranean boats, has been imitated in a globular arrangement
of rope yarns. Arab, Persian and Indian vessels likewise have been
described as being adorned with animal skins, sometimes dyed blood-
red, fastened to the stemhead. James Hornell has interpreted such
"fleeces" as symbolizing animal sacrifices made during the launching
ceremonies.*

*119 Votive tablet from 1609 in the church of the Madonna dell'Arco
at Naples. This church, like numerous other shore-side churches in the
Mediterranean, was richly endowed with votive donations from the
seagoing population, given in accordance with the deeply religious
feeling of the people and in fulfillment of vows made at the occasion of
salvation from distress at sea. Each of the little scenes painted on
wood has an inscription explaining the event, to which are usually
added the letters VFGA (*Votum fecit, gratiam accepti: he made a
vow and received grace*). Some of the votive tablets were painted by
the sailors themselves, some by special painters, the Madonnari.*

120 In the seamen's churches one also finds votive statues besides the tablets. This baroque angel with the barge broken in half (in the rapids of the Danube) used to stand in a chapel near Linz in Upper Austria.

121 Wilhelm Marstrand (1810–1873): Going to church in Leksand (Sweden). Oil painting, 1853.
In Norway, Sweden and Finland there were special feast day boats for going to church on the holidays. These vessels belonged to a village boat community, whose members shared in the duties and privileges concerning the boat. Every household belonging to the community was responsible for one of the fourteen oars and identified it with its own mark. During the annual meetings of the company the oarsman's place for each family was decided upon. The church-going boats of Dalarne, one of which, from the year 1716, is on view in the Stockholm Skansen Museum, had names like "The Feast", "The Crown", "Hawk", "Wolf", "Fox" or "Flea". It was traditional to race the boats on the holiday ride to church.

122 *Eye ornaments at the bow of a fishing boat on the Portuguese Atlantic coast.*

Right:
123 *Eye ornaments at the bow of a Yugoslavian coast freighter in the Adriatic port of Split in Dalmatia, 1965.*

In the huge regions between the Mediterranean and India, East Africa and Southeast Asia, China and the northwest coast of America, this most remarkable of all traditional decorative ship insignia continues to be used. Oculi of this kind were accentuating the bows of vessels as early as the bronze age civilization of ancient Egypt; later, the Cretans, Etruscans, Greeks and Romans used eye-shaped designs, as did the seamen of Hindu India. The ornament is interpreted as a protection against the "evil eye"; also as a luck charm or simply to look out for the true course. Developed 6000 years ago from magical concepts that had their roots in the very real need for security of the bronze age sailors whose understanding and control of natural forces was after all of a low order, the anti-sorcery symbol proved to be uncommonly resistant to the changes wrought by the various state religions which succeeded one another, and has remained alive in these regions, although often in modified form.

124 At Whitsuntide the fishermen of Kölpinsee on the Baltic island of Usedom tie a bouquet of birch branches to the mast trucks of their beach boats. Symbolic signs in many forms are still used today by northern European fishermen and sailors in their boats and are part of traditional custom: a cross or greenery at the mast truck; a star, heart, cloverleaf or horseshoe at the stemhead. Some, like the Pentecostal bouquet of new foliage, may be remnants of ancient traditions. Others, e.g. placing a Christmas tree in the boat, are quite new. When inquiring into the age and origin of such signs it is helpful to remember that such observations should be related to regional and social conditions of communal life. But it is as well to know something about boats too: three nails projecting outward from the mast truck are not a "sign" but a device to prevent seabirds from roosting.

125 *The crew of a Danish fishing cutter in their quarters.*

The rule according to which the various sections of the ship were each allocated a purpose expressed the partnership principle: the entire vessel belonged to everybody. A division of the deck area into a region "before the mast" and another one "aft" was not practiced any more than a distinction between forecastle and cabin. The ship's cuddy, below the quarterdeck, usually low of ceiling and poorly lighted, was for everyone. The furniture consisted of stove, table and benches, the sleeping accommodation was a straw mattress in a bunk—the same for every man. In open vessels there was a hearth on a bed of sand or stones, or the cooking was done over a fire lit and maintained in a capacious fire pot half filled with ashes, as was the custom in the old *Elbjollen* (yawl boats of the Elbe). The menu for all three shipboard meals was under the rule of fresh fish, together with bread, bacon, gruel, peas and beans, a diet ridiculed by the old rhyme aimed at the Oderhaff skipper: "Fellows, eat fish, potatoes cost money!" The customary beverage on board in the old times was a light, top-fermented ship's beer. The use of hot coffee became general in North Germany and Scandinavia only toward the end of the 18th century. At meal times, the first scoop from the large wooden serving bowl, the *Back*, was either the standing privilege of the senior crew member, or else every member took his turn for one day. Every man had a little earthenware dish both for eating and drinking, called the *Kumm*. The *Back* and a spoon for each man were part of the ship's inventory.

The working dress was the same for all the ship's company—a sight especially fascinating to the 19th-century marine painters (ill. 126). The fabrics were chiefly home-spun linen, sheep's wool and cowhide. The dress consisted of linen shirts, knitted woolen singlets, woolen tights pulled up above the hips, knee-length woolen socks; scarves and caps likewise of wool. The upper garment was a long woolen vest and wide linen trousers, over which a linen frock or jacket was worn, as well as a long, leather work apron. Not rarely, the sailors made these "togs" for themselves, for they were entirely at home with the adept use of net-knitting needles as well as with the sail-maker's tools. Some of the articles of wear customary with sailors in foreign-going ships were largely unknown in the coastal trade. For instance, these sailors preferred wooden clogs to sea boots, which earned them the nickname of "Träsko skipper" from the Scandinavian *trä sko* (wooden shoe), once a familiar appellation over all northern Europe. Another characteristical professional emblem was the woolen double-thumbed mitten.

Inseparably connected with the work partnership on board are the popular nicknames and epithets bestowed on boats as readily as on crew members, whether designating a specific vessel in a fleet of similar local types, or an individual from out of a group of people with the same family name. We encounter terms like the "Pregnant Woman" for a tubby, rotund vessel, "Grease Pan" after the part of an old-fashioned launching slip which dispensed tallow and tar, or the "Snake", "Flea" and "Baldy" which are self-explanatory, or "Chuck the Criminal", the "Little Dane" of Hiddensee, "The American" of the Hel (Hela) peninsula. Horn and bell signals, blasts on a whistle, wordless shouts and rhythmic work-songs with solo and chorus, had their distinct signalling and coordinating function, and had surely served as such in the ancient communal shipboard groups as means of communication between working sections. Not without reason do some of the most impressive of work-songs survive today in communities formerly organized along these lines—whether on Heligoland or Hiddensee—for example, in the communal act of hauling the boats onto the beach.

Everyday working life on board in the North Sea and Baltic areas in the 19th century was still permeated to an extraordinary extent by traditional ritual customs and beliefs. Doubtless the elements of many of these had been in use for long periods of time, although the ritual act as such may have changed form. Often we find words, gestures and symbols in conjunction, notably in the many examples of defensive magic known from the Baltic coastal regions, for instance the presumably disaster-arresting effect of the presence of naked steel on board, be it sailmakers' needles ("three eyes see more than two"), blades of hatchets and knives, or horseshoes. Almost all aspects of ship work were wreathed about with taboos, to which belongs the prohibition of departure during the noon hour or on a Monday or Friday, and also of molesting of certain species of birds that had alighted on board, e.g. the wagtail, the albatross, etc. Injunctions reported from Estonia, forbade lies and deceit, envy and hatred, fighting and theft, so long as the boat's company are together.

Sacrificial acts, thought to have the virtue of propitiating fortune, were numerous in coastal as well as in inland navigation. The custom of placing coins in the mast step belongs in this category, and the antiquity of this custom is shown by a coin found thus placed in the wreck-find at Blackfriars (London) (2nd century). Along the Oderhaff, the coin was placed in a peg-hole of the sternpost, a sacred spot since ancient times. The fishermen of Kurski Saliv (Courland lagoon) deposited a sacrificial offering at the cutwater of their boats, consisting of bread, salt and so-called "snake water", a liquid distilled out of the cadaver of a snake. Another ritual believed to bring about lucky voyages was the annual sacrifice of a wreath of foliage and berries of the mountain ash, which was cast into the waters of the lagoon. Besides magic, taboos and sacrificial offerings, there was the broad area of mantic mysticism, the devining of events to come. As this prophesying centered almost exclusively around weather predictions, it is understandable that this art once had extreme importance. Having attained but a moderate level of comprehension of natural phenomena, sailors believed it to be necessary to appease supernatural powers in order to dispose them favorably toward their fishing and navigational activities. In this realm belongs the interpretation of the action of those fluorescent light effects sometimes seen at masthead or yardarm, the so-called St. Elmo's Fire; and the custom for the helmsman to salute the moon by raising his cap to it, when relieving the wheel at the change of watch, is likewise a propitiatory act.

Of course the partnership work of the ship's company in our latitudes was also accompanied by Christian rituals. From medieval times we know of impressive benedictions, including the singing of psalms, prayers, sprinkling with holy water and reading of the gospels. The traditional signal for departure: "In the Name of God, let us depart!" is chronicled from the 13th century. Especially from those coasts of northern Europe which remained Catholic after the Reformation—in the southern Baltic the coastal strip between the ports of Puck (Putzig) and Tolkmicko (Tolkemit); in the West the Channel coast between Flanders and Brittany, and all of Ireland— we know of very varied examples of blessings both for departure and homecoming, of boat processions, votive gifts in the shape of pictures, statues and ship models, and of the use of Christian symbols outside and within the ship. Prayer ceremonials and ritual gestures while fishing have been recorded in Heligoland and Norderney.

From the same places also come instances of the custom of carving devotional mottoes in the thwarts of boats:

"May the Lord preserve
Those who the Crowned Angel serve!"

In fishing boats of the southern Baltic coasts, the following verses were found:

"God guides the seaman   "In storm and weather
But steer, he must himself."   God is my savior."

Many religious seagoing hymns are obviously of very ancient origin, such as those mentioned in an account of the Cassubian fishermen of the Hel (Hela) peninsula: "During the voyage they sing their church hymns almost without intermission ... when at last the harbor is sighted, they sail into the calm water of the landing giving thanks to God."

126 Wilhelm Krause (1803–1864): Southern Italian fishing boat's crew. Drawing, about 1842.

Women Working on Board

The fact of women collaborating in fishing and navigation constitutes a special variant of the communal work of partners with equal rights on board ship. This variant appears on the scene in several distinct forms, which can be related to specific levels of social evolution. Unfortunately, this fascinating theme has remained almost totally unexplored in European ethnography. Brief notes concerning the fishing in company of men and women come from Finland, Estonia, Courland (Kurzeme) and the southern Baltic coast, and from Heligoland. This kind of shipboard collaboration does not necessarily represent a relic of primitive social conditions. It has often happened, for example, that the hardships of wars lasting for decades have made a permanent institution out of an originally temporary emergency situation.

A very ancient form of the division of labor is represented by the boating done by women of island and marsh farms, which continues in our time in the Swedish and Finnish skerries and on the shores of the Oder lagoon. Traditionally, the women's share in farm work, cattle grazing and feeding, watering and milking, and haymaking, necessitates trips by water to and from the pastures and may thus be viewed as being an environmentally imposed condition. Formerly, the women and girls rowed, nowadays they are motorized; but it is their portion, the men being engaged in fishing meanwhile, or doing other work. A classic example of such rustic female navigation exists in the inland Spreewald.

Journeys of the wives and daughters of fishermen to the fish markets of the vicinity, which are, or were, common practice on both sides of the southern Baltic, probably date back to early feudal times when castles of the nobility, seaports and episcopal seats were founded, of which the fishing settlements were dependencies.

Relics of ancient customs and exceptional situations, such as we have presented in the foregoing, by no means exhaust the cases of female collaboration on board. The role of European women as workers in vessels saw its most effective development in the North Sea and Baltic coastwise navigation and in the inland cargo-carrying trade between the Schelde and the Niemen (Memel). The development is probably due to early capitalist conditions of the 16th and 17th centuries, at least in the Netherlands and Flanders. From these adjacent western countries, this form of female labor penetrated during the 19th century into Northwest German coastwise shipping, for instance East Friesian village navigation, where it was manifestly due to the economic pressure of the capitalist social structure. Lübbert Lübbers stated this clearly in 1903: "Our coastwise sailors can protect themselves against the competition of the Dutch traders only through following their example, in taking their families on board in order to save wages." It has not yet been possible to decide whether the other existing center of female shipboard labor—the canal and river routes between the Elbe, Havel and Oder, branching as far as Pregolja (Pregel) and Niemen (Memel)—is also to be ascribed to Dutch influence, or whether it stems from work habits originating in the East. At present, the painting showing barge people of the Spree river at Berlin, by Adolph von Menzel from 1867, is the oldest known documentation from the area under discussion. In the organizations of bargemen and coastwise sailors, which were, for the most part, founded only in the 19th century, the wives accompanying their husbands on board did not have equal rights. This seems to indicate that here too the beginnings of female collaboration occurred under the aegis of capitalist changes in the mode of living. During the age of feudalism, the women who were active in the transporting and marketing of cargos of fish enjoyed regular membership standing in the northeast German fishermen's guilds.

127 Hermann Schweffel: Fisher women from Ellerbeck at the quay of the Kiel fish market. Watercolor, about 1900. Boat trips made by the women to the town market were still characteristic in many fishing villages in northern Europe in the early 20th century.

128 *Women of the Melanesian Lau fishing population gathering sea urchins.*

The Lau live in isolated groups on islets erected by themselves out of coral blocks, off Malaita in the Solomon Islands. They have a language of their own and strange customs. Despite a clearly marked, archaic division of labor—while the men are fishing, the women gather clams, crustaceans and spiny mollusks and also do the marketing—women no less than men are skilled in handling boats. The women paddle, but the men mostly propel the boats by poling from a standing position, while the vessel is in shallow water. Lau children, too, become familiar with water craft at an early age. In the Far East, the women of the Japanese-Korean Ama fishing population were well known as divers for clams and edible seaweed. The Ama belonged to the less privileged groups of the "maritime pariah".

129 Eduard Hildebrandt (1818–1869):
Fishing settlement with boat dwellings
off Macao. Watercolor, 1864.

130 Eduard Hildebrandt:
Boats of Hongkong. Watercolor, 1863.

ABLE SEAMAN

Left:

131 Portrait. Oil painting of the North Friesian master of a sloop, Marten Mathiessen of Fanø, 1806.

132 Sailorly self-portrayal, engraving on sperm whale tooth. "Scrimshaw" was especially popular with the whalers of New England. It is regarded as the only truly indigenous major North American folk art, excepting Indian and Eskimo art.

Gli Marinari per inueterato Costume fanno in certi passaggi all'hor che iui peruengono una ceremonia ridicola, da loro abusiuamente chiamato Battesimo, in segno d'allegrezza d'hauere terminato felicemente il uiaggio, e per rapire la mancia da qualche inesperto Passaggiere.

133 The oldest known representation of the Equatorial baptism,
aboard a French ship.
From V. M. Coronelli, Atlante Veneto, Venice 1690.

134 *Equatorial baptismal
certificate for the ship's engineer
Wilhelm Lücke of Ückermünde,
on board the German steamer
"Prinz Waldemar", 1905.*

135 *The 15-men crew of the bark "Danmark" of Copenhagen (1898). Pictures like this used to be part of the souvenirs of every deep-water sailor.*

What were the living and working conditions a seaman's wife might find, when going aboard one of the common local small cargo sailers of the Oderhaff, say around 1890 or 1900? Unlike in the Netherlands, these vessels had not been civilized by generations of women forming a regular part of the ship's company: they were purely "male" boats, and they looked the part. The so-called *Bude* (living quarters), situated either below the foredeck or aft, was at best some 4 meters long and perhaps 1.5 meters high. Besides the companion ladder stood the range made of firebrick masonry, or sometimes, in its place, a factory-made "cooking machine" of sheet metal. Instead of the men's bunks, a broad bed stood alongside the cabin wall. Opposite were a clothes closet, washstand and dish closet; table and chairs were ranged against the bed, or else (if forward) in the angle of the bow. A kerosene lamp was suspended from the skylight. That was all. A woman entering such a community had to resign herself to the absence of a good many facilities which were a matter of course even then in the rustic living conditions on shore, especially in regard to sanitary conditions. This was the milieu in which the work year, from Easter to Christmas, had to be lived through, without regard to heat or cold, gales, days of continual rain or weeks of fog.

Life on board the coasters, more than once characterized by old skippers as a dog's life, was made more worthy of human dignity by the sailors' wives. They cooked three or four meals a day, baked a cake for Sunday, washed the linen and fired the stove. When they arrived on board, the living quarters were cleaned up and kept that way; pictures found their way onto the cabin walls, lamps and door handles were polished; a flower vase was put in, a table cloth and curtains at the port holes. The skipper no longer needed to spend lonesome hours at the helm—day or night—with his dog for sole company. Ships with women on board could be recognized at a distance from the window boxes on deck, planted with kitchen herbs and flowers, and from the presence of domestic animals, a dog, cat or canary bird, chickens or rabbits.

The duties of sailors' wives combined domestic obligations with regular seamen's work. They worked as deckhands: mooring and unmooring, raising the anchor, hoisting sails. In earlier times they helped to load and unload cargo. They steered as a matter of course; some women were better helmsmen than their husbands. They knew the winds and weather, were familiar with buoys, beacons and lighthouses; they were at home with harbor entrances, mooring berths and anchoring grounds of their cruising area. But they were also acquainted with all the ship chandlers, butchers and bakers in the vicinity; they knew where to go for the best drinking water. After the First World War, when bureaucracy reached out into everyday life and thus also into the coastwise trade, it was mostly the skippers' wives who became the book-keepers of these microscopic "businesses". A little later, motorization began in earnest and even here, some of the women did not flinch at the proposition of servicing those cast-iron monsters of now obsolete hot-bulb motors and their blustering blow torches.

Command Structure

Walther Vogel, in his "Geschichte der deutschen See-schiffahrt" points out a change in the designations for shipmasters in documents of the 13th century. Where previously the master was referred to as *gubernator* or *styreman*, after 1250 more and more frequently the terms *dominus navis* or *scip her* or *skipper*, are encountered. The significant transition from a state of social partnership to the feudal command structure within the ship's company thus becomes linguistically focussed. The most likely reason for the change is that, with the beginnings of the feudal social order, the vessels of the northern European coastal trade were no longer the common property of partners, but were owned either by single persons or, if by a partnership group, by persons no longer doing ship's work themselves. The "ship's children", subordinate to the command of the skipper, were hired and paid for a certain, given period; or they were remunerated on the basis of earning a percentage of the profits. The system of signing on a crew for a fishing or coasting voyage on the basis of a sliding scale of shares in the profit of the voyage, according to the services performed by each individual, was still in common use during the first half of this century in northern Europe. A last remnant of the old right of co-optation of the partnerships is visible in the institution of the ship's council, which consisted of master, mates and all hands, and whose authority in cases of sea emergencies was still recognized by the Hamburg Sea Law of 1497.

The division of seagoing ships into deck areas "before the mast" and "quarterdeck" was only known since the early epoch of urban-civic sea trading. The sailors' dwelling was "before the mast"; they had no right to be "aft" without the call of duty, for that was the area where the master had his living quarters, later also the mates; likewise, the merchant, who in the early times often came along on the voyage, was quartered there. Thus it remained for centuries. Although around the middle of the 19th century the living quarters of the men were transferred in most sailing ships from the forecastle below decks to the forward deckhouse, after the American example, the sailors did not realize much of an improvement of their standard of living. The deckhouse of the barkentine "Hoppet", built in 1878 and now in the Stockholm Marine-Historical Museum, may serve as illustration of conditions. The house is 4.5 meters long by 4 meters wide; its location was between fore and main mast and it was entered from aft, through a transversely partitioned "Dutch" door. Oilskins were hung and seaboots removed in the entry. Next the entry was the galley, fitted with an iron range with five cooking places and a baking oven. In the adjoining living quarters, along the walls, were two double bunks, with berths for four sleepers. Before the bunks were the sea chests of the men, which also served as seats. A fixed table was fastened to the front wall. Daylight came in through a skylight that could be hinged open. At night, a kerosene lamp, suspended from the ceiling, illuminated the room. There was no heating stove, heat being provided only through the open door of the galley. The thin boards of the deckhouse walls gave very poor insulation against heat and cold, but they did shelter a sufficient quantity of the familiar tormentors that made a hell for the men in hot summer nights: when the starboard side of the deckhouse was broken up, in 1966, to be replaced by a glass pane, thick layers of dead bedbugs were found.

Conditions were materially different on the quarterdeck, as evidenced by the cabin of the Swedish barkentine "Ziba" (of 1876), on exhibit in the same museum. In the after deckhouse, besides the provision room, were two staterooms for the mates, with washstands, and the captain's quarters, with writing desk and chart locker. Between these three cabins was the messroom or dining room of the afterguard. It was furnished with table, chairs and a sofa, as well as a dish cupboard. Everything was more substantially built, cheerfully painted, better ventilated, better lighted and, above all, heated.

The sanitary installations for the men before the mast corresponded to the living quarters. As late as the mid-19th century, ships had neither washing facilities nor a toilet for the crew. Everybody did the best he could. This may help to explain why many seamen were not overly fastidious in matters of personal hygiene while on board. After copious rainfalls, when quantities of fresh water were collected, great laundry days were celebrated. Shaving was often deferred until one had shore leave. A haircut —confined to the neck, along the rim of a cooking vessel capsized over the head—was performed by a shipmate, whose fee might be getting some help in washing his clothes.

The particular details of the sailor dress in the European-North American merchant service: short lined jacket or frock made of thick blue woolen cloth, blue shirt of linen with broad collar, knotted kerchief, wide blue wool or white linen trousers, sea boots, oilskins and sou'wester became general only since the end of the 18th century, partly through the influence of naval service. Previously, work clothes worn at sea were the same as ashore. An indispensable piece of equipment was the sheath knife worn on the belt. Personal belongings were kept and carried about in the sea bag and sea chest, of which mention is made already in the Middle Ages.

Regarding the food on board, chapters instead of a few lines would have to be written. The story would have to begin with the introduction of the fixed ship's hearth made of masonry, which decidedly contributed to the betterment of living conditions. We know neither when this happened, nor whom we have to thank for it. One feels tempted to speculate that the invention came from the Flanders-Friesian region. Here and there, as late as the 19th century, cooking was done on deck over an open fire, in a cooking house fitted with an iron tripod. The funnel construction was problematical. Reinier Nooms' etchings of 1650 show chimneys of masonry; later, tin stovepipes came into use.

The provisioning of seagoing vessels was in all periods determined by the problem of food preservation. Since the Middle Ages we know of the alternating menu of salt meat and salt fish. To add fat to the diet, smoked bacon was used. Also attested since medieval times is the twice-baked hard bread of seamen, the home of the weevil. Side dishes were peas and beans, also much barley gruel and groats, with dried fruit and a "duff" on Sundays. Fresh water had to be rationed most carefully. Sailors are indebted to a parsimonious British admiral for the invention of watering rum or arrack into what became known as grog. Three hot meals were standard in northern European vessels, but from the proverbs of sailormen one can see that regional variations of quantity and quality existed: Scandinavians and Dutchmen ate five meals a day, and good ones at that, while in general the many different German flags were known as hunger flags, and were therefore unpopular.

Problems of provisioning could be kept at a bearable level as long as the voyage was in home waters or in the vicinity of land. The danger began with months-long, world-wide ocean voyages, where the mute partner whose name was scurvy—pathological vitamin deficiency—was constantly threatening. Dutch and English shipowners combatted the danger of scurvy from the beginning, partly with sauerkraut, partly with lemon juice, and also by taking on board whole herds of live cattle. In England, the wholesome lemon juice was often replaced by the cheaper, though less effective, lime juice, whence British vessels bore the name of "limejuicers" to the end of sailing-ship days. The first English and French patents for the conserving of foodstuffs in glass or tin containers date from 1810, but it was not until 1852 that the Royal Navy was able to open its own canned goods factory. Subsequently canned foods were gradually introduced into the merchant marine, in which advance, however, shipowners did not evince undue haste.

Against this background of often depressing housing, sanitary and nutritional conditions the shipboard life of the men before the mast carried on in the steady rhythm of much work and little leisure, without any possibility of a free unfolding and almost without the right to an existence worthy of human beings.

The organization of labor on board the larger vessels was probably established since the Middle Ages according to various fixed schedules. The sailors were divided in two "quarters" or watches, each group under the command of a mate (chief and second) whose responsibility it was to see that the commands given by the captain were executed, but whose privileges included permission to give orders on his own. Three specialists—cook, sailmaker and carpenter—might be freed from regular watch duty by the captain and employed at specific tasks. Under normal conditions all work was done by the watch on deck, whose tour of duty was four hours; the port watch being under the command of the first officer, the starboard watch under the second mate. But in any emergency when the command was *all hands!* the watch below lost their rest period.

Walther Vogel voices the opinion that in the 13th and 14th centuries there were no recognizable gradations of rank among the ship's company. The complete nautical grade scale formed at some later period, its various ranks being based on experience, although without a corresponding repartition of work responsibilities. At the bottom of the ladder is the ship's boy; on subsequent levels we find the novice, ordinary seaman, able-bodied seaman and boatswain. The sailors jealously observed the ritualistic respect due this hierarchy, which reminds one of the guild spirit. It regulated aspects of life in the forecastle, observance of behavioral rules at meal times, etc. It was Order in the feudal sense.

Ship work has always been of two kinds; there is the work directly connected with the ship's movements—making sail, trimming and bracing, reefing and furling, working the ground tackle, manning the helm—and there is maintenance and repair work, the care of running and standing rigging, sail mending and patching, the care of deck and hull. The hierarchy made it possible to find occasion, particularly in the second category of ship's work, for endless, often senseless, sometimes positively cruel occupation for subordinates one wished to punish. Especially hated by all sailors was the continuous pumping in old, wooden vessels; also, in iron ships, the chipping of rust from the interior.

All group actions dealing with the ship's progress through the water—heaving in of the anchor, hoisting sail, bracing the yards—but in the category of maintenance work only the working of the pumps, were executed in the old-time sailing ships in rhythmical physical exertions. To help to keep time, these were accompanied by work-songs, which are typical for this professional group and have been traced back to the 16th century. They have become widely familiar under the name of shanties (ill. 136, 137), and consist of alternating parts: a solo by the leader, a chorus by the work gang. The shantyman sings his animating, encouraging, preferably improvised and a thousand-fold varied line; the group answers in unison with the time-setting refrain ending in a work shout. As a vocal genre, the shanty certainly originated through variations and amplifications of the work shouts of sailors. The older, nationally distinct texts have been obsolete for a long time. The shanty language, during the 18th and 19th centuries, became exclusively a slangy English spoken by sailors. There is no set form, immutable and observed, for these true folk songs. In their infinite variety they entered the worldwide tradition of sailormen and disappeared together with them and their environment, the big blue-water sailing ships.

Oh, whiskey is the life of man,
oh, whiskey, Johnny,

Oh, I'll drink whiskey when I can—
oh, whiskey for my Johnny.

Oh, whiskey is the life of man,
oh, whiskey from an old tin can.

Oh, whiskey hot and whiskey cold,
oh, whiskey new and whiskey old.

Oh, whiskey killed my poor old Dad,
oh, whiskey drove my mother mad.

Oh, whiskey made me pawn my clothes,
oh, whiskey gave me this red nose.

Oh, whiskey is the life of man,
oh, I'll drink whiskey when I can.

I thought I heard the Old Man say:
oh, whiskey for all hands!—Belay!

Halyard- and capstan shanty
(possibly 16th century)

Despite the division of labor into shipmaster and deck crew, there was not, on the whole, in the Middle Ages, a difference in educational background in the two classes. As late as 1540 the Swiss mathematician Georg Rhaeticus noted, during a visit to the southern Baltic coast, "Many shipmen sailing toward England or Portugal from Prussia do not use *latitudinibus* (method of determining latitudes) and likewise esteem not sea charts nor a true compass. For, as they boast, they carry their art in their head." This experiential professional knowledge, passed on by word of mouth from one generation to the next, was the common property of the deck crew as much as of the steersmen. Men of both groups were equally able to handle the ancient, traditional instruments of navigation: the lead, the half-hour glass, the compass. The basic component of the com-pass, the magnet, had been known in European navigation since the times of the Vikings. About 1300 the instrument was much improved for practical shipboard use through the combination of the pointer with a compass card, and through the invention of a universally moveable suspension in a protective housing. In the Mediterranean the compass was used to steer by, but it is probable that in the north of Europe it was used only for taking bearings and for time calculations of the turning of the tides.

The progress of emancipation of the northern European bourgeoisie, which increased rapidly during the period of full-blown feudalism, brought with it significant cultural changes. Not the least of these was the unfolding of the bourgeois educational system, thanks to which, in the course of the 16th century, reading and writing became the common property of the urban middle classes. Shipmasters and officers belonged to this class, and this is the reason why from this period on we see them emerging above the foremast hands, i.e. on the grounds of better education. One of the first concrete indications of this new situation was the use of handwritten sailing directions, the origin of which, in the Mediterranean area, is presumed to be as early as the 13th century. In the South such "portolanes" were soon illustrated with pictorial maps oriented toward north and showing the 32 divisions of the compass card. The North European "sea books" were a little more frugally decorated; they were first used in Flanders whence they spread, during the 15th century, through northern France and England as well as the Low German Hanseatic regions. After the invention of printing, this late medieval information service improved in quality. The oldest printed portolane was published in Venice in 1490 under the following title: "Questa e una opera necessaria a tutti li naviganti." About 1510 the North European sailing directory "Le grant Routtier" was printed, the compiler being the French shipmaster Pierre Garcie. The Dutch published their first printed sailing directory at Amsterdam in 1532; it was decorated with woodcut illustrations showing characteristic coastal views.

But all this is a mere prologue to coming changes. The real revolution in nautical affairs stemmed from the demands which the traversing of vast ocean spaces made on shipmasters, necessitating other aids than sailing directions for home waters, and an acquaintance with terrestrial navigation and determining a ship's position from coastal landmarks. On the high seas the daily position had to be calculated from observation of the heavenly bodies, and courses were set toward unfamiliar latitudes. Oral information, which had so far been the only means of handing down knowledge, had been good enough for thousands of years, but it would not do for the study of geometry and arithmetics. A new approach was created in Portugal: shortly after 1500 there appeared, in Évora, the first manual of astronomical navigation, the "Regimento do estrolabio e do quadrante". In 1545 appeared the work of the Spaniard Pedro de Medina, whose "Arte de Navegar" became universally famous and within a short period after publication was translated into French, Italian, English and Dutch. In the Netherlands and in England in particular, the ambitious bourgeoisie strove to match the Iberian leaders. Cornelis Anthonisz of Amsterdam printed his "Onderwijsinge om stuermanschap te leeren" in 1544; William Bourne of London issued his "Regiment for the Sea" in 1574. Renowned scholars labored to perfect scientific navigation: in 1533 Gemma Frisius described the geometrical method of angular measurement; Georg Rhaeticus was the first to publish, in 1551, all six trigonometric tables of angular functions. Simon Stevin used the decimal system in 1585; John Napier in 1614 invented logarithms, which slightly later were improved by Henry Briggs and Adrian Vlacq to the extent where they could be used in practical navigation. In 1625 the British seacaptain Thomas Addison published the first textbook in which astronomical navigation problems were solved logarithmically. The Dutch were especially given to the use of copper engravings for illustrating nautical charts and sailing directories, Lucas Waghenaers' "Spieghel der Zeevaert" of 1584 being a good example. To conclude this outline of rapid progress in navigational techniques, we will mention that all the previously lacking instruments—the ship's log, reflector goniometer (octant), telescope, barometer and chronometer—which are used to this day in ocean navigation, were invented or perfected in this period.

Formal nautical academic training began in England in 1598 with the first public civil course in navigation, offered at London Grasham College, followed very quickly by similar professional schools in the Netherlands. The invention of the modern chronometer by John Harrison in 1736 solved the last great problem of ocean navigation, i.e. exact time and longitude determination. From this time on, the precious measuring instruments such as chronometer and sextant, became nautical status symbols (ill. 131). Their ownership and the ability to handle them have, ever since, identified any sailor of the European and North American merchant marine as belonging to a stratum to which one rose not because of factors of birth or influential marriage, but solely through the merit of years of practical navigational experience. From the 17th century on, the social status of the inhabitants of the northern European urbanized and culturally emancipated seafarers' villages was determined by nautical skills and abilities, and no longer by real estate.

136 Stan Hugill: At the Pumps. Undated drawing. The English seaman Stan Hugill became known in 1961 through his voluminous collection of shanties.

137 The oldest known German notation of a shanty which was "sung" by the sailors when they had to keep time for hard work calling for pulling or lifting in unison. The poet Nikolaus Lenau (1802–1850) took this note in a Dutch sailing-ship during a transatlantic passage, and later gave the sheet, unfortunately without a text, to a friend who passed it along to the Swabian poet Justinus Kerner in 1850.

Watch Below and Harbor Life

During daylight hours, when not on duty, sailors had to find ways to amuse themselves; climate and weather permitting on deck, otherwise in their quarters. Sleep during the day was difficult because of the unceasing commotion; the lack of space on deck did not invite constitutional exercises. The cramped forecastle was too dark and too noisy to do much reading, apart from the fact that until after the First World War reading matter for sailors was dull and in short supply. The humidity of the air, moreover, quickly mildewed even the Bibles donated by the seamen's missions. From the beginning of the 1920s cheap paperbacks and adventure magazines, passed from hand to hand, provided some kind of entertainment.

What was there left to do with the free time? Jack Tar made use of his matchless manual skill. Ship models were whittled and rigged up in bottles (ill. 139). The sailors made woodwork from scraps—footstools, sewing boxes and little cupboards, the covers of which were ornamented with carvings or inlaid work. The interior surfaces of the lids of sea chests were decorated with paintings; men knitted, crocheted, embroidered ship portraits, sewed tobacco pouches and ditty bags; they braided mats, drawstrings for sea bags, handles for sea chests, bell ropes for the ship's bell, and similar fancy work. More famous objects are the scrimshaw engravings on whales' teeth and whalebone, made mostly but not exclusively by the crews of whalers and sealing vessels (ill. 132). The creation of these objects aboard the deepwatermen in the 19th century amounts to a real folk art of international, not regional, scope. They were made of the same materials and in the same style the world over. Only the ornamental elements and background motifs retained details of more local interest.

These products of leisure were made partly to help pass the time, of course. The thought of making a present to bring back to the folks at home, or even the hope of turning an honest penny with the sale of some successful piece, also counts as a motivation. But it is also certain that all this "scrimshandering" (Melville) somehow expresses a deeper stratum of the individual; secret and half-conscious longings and desires. A last remnant of privacy is affirmed by the individual decoration of a sea chest. Some specimens of fancy work represent a tour de force, as though the artist were seeking some proof of his worth in living up to the truth of the slogan "There is nothing a sailorman can't do!"—Speaking of this slogan, it is too bad that it applied only to manual dexterity; in a social sense, it is not true, for the 19th-century sailor was incapable of changing his lot to any degree. His knots and splices might be perfect; on shore, he might present a "ship-shape" appearance, dress in what he might think to be the latest English fashions; he might succeed in scandalizing the burghers with his tobacco chewing, his tattooings and his slang; his impersonation of his specialty might be perfect: "Jack Tar"—Jan Maat—at home in any port the world over. But on board he had no individuality, no possibility of unfolding his personality. He remained a subordinate. If he was called to the poop, he had to come with cap in hand. The closest he could hope to come to genteel food, like the chicken broth destined for the officer's mess, would be to steal it from the galley. Discounting his admitted right to growl—"Growl you may, but go you must"—there was no self-assertion for the man before the mast, neither toward the captain and mates, nor against the senior ranks amongst the sailors. So long as the ship was on the high seas, the seaman was in the legal power of the captain "body and soul".

Dammed-up aggressions and protest sought an escape valve in another form of leisure activity: the wild play of tough men. In boxing and wrestling they found an outlet for their frustrations, which were still more savagely or even cruelly manifested in their fishing for sharks and porpoises and their hunting of ship's rats. Aggression was also at the bottom of the many seagoing hazing rites and playing of tricks, that formed part of the customary ceremonials at the occasion of crossing certain boundaries of traditional cruising grounds: at the mouth of Oder and Thames, for instance, or at the exit of the Öre Sound, or passing Gibraltar. The baptismal rites of southern-going voyages, i.e. the crossing of the "Line" (the Equator), which has been traced back to the middle of the 16th century (ill. 133), were apt to degenerate into sadistic tormenting of helpless victims, in keeping with the shipboard hierarchy which winked at liberties being taken with weaker members of the crew and underdogs in general, such as men of other races or religions who often formed part of the international mixed crews of most ships in the deepwater trade.

138 Vaisseau fontôme, *phantom ship, is the title of this Flemish etching of about 1500. It is viewed as proof of the existence of an ancient prototype of sailors' legends concerning disastrous encounters with spectral ships (probably drifting wrecks), which during the 17th and 18th centuries gradually evolved into the myth of the "Flying Dutchman".*

Of course, there were also more harmless games in off-duty hours: cards, chess and checkers, dancing and agility contests. Vocalists performed languishing love-songs, violin or accordion produced sentimental melodies and were greatly enjoyed—and of course there was the great re-source of "spinning a yarn" or storytelling, such as the accounts of voyages "jinxed" by an unlucky crew mem-ber—the "Jonas"—or the legends of the *Klabauter-mann*" (ship's goblin). Unlimited licence was granted to cheerful lying, virtuosity in the presentation of tall tales being especially appreciated. The so-called "sailor myths" on the other hand probably originated largely on shore, with a few exceptions dealing with noteworthy events of past voyages, for instance encounters with drifting derelicts (ill. 138).

The numerous feasts and holidays of shore life had next to no part in the life on board the blue-water ships of the 18th and 19th centuries. Only Christmas and Good Friday were observed, conditions permitting. Many captains marked Sunday with somewhat better food and an extra allowance of fresh water, or through the remission of senseless tasks; possibly also with a sermon, which might be crowned with schnapps all round. In "good" ships an ancient custom was observed in serving a somewhat better meal on Thursdays as well.

The watch below was also the time to apply to the cap-tain for medical care. Many sea captains rivalled in practical knowledge of diagnosis and practical surgery the skill of an average country doctor, and disposed of a well-stocked medicine chest. The first textbook for practical seagoing medicine appeared in 1693 in London, the "Chirurgus marinus" by Moyle. The first German work of this kind,

139 G. T. Schulz: Sailing-ship seamen making a bottle ship-model during the watch below in the forecastle.
Drawing from: Unter Segeln rund Kap Horn, Hamburg 1956.

the "Dietetic-Medical Handbook for Seamen" by Friedrich Henning, published in 1800, was in common shipboard use for decades. Unfortunately the occupational diseases of sailors which resulted from unfavorable living conditions afloat, primarily rheumatism, gout, effects of vitamin deficiency and stomach ailments, could not be combatted with any but insufficient effect with the resources of the medicine chest. On the other hand many sailors' lives were saved through the conscientious care of a responsible skipper, in cases of fracture, dislocation, bruises or burns. When help had failed, one of the few interruptions of work afloat arrived: the time for a ritual hallowed by tradition. The corpse was laid to rest in the sea, shrouded in the flag of his home country while the vessel, with yards aback if she was a sailing ship, with engines stopped if a steamer, flag at half staff, briefly halted on her course and the captain read the burial service from the Bible, followed by the Lord's Prayer, after which the men sang a hymn, perhaps the favorite of the deceased comrade.

Whether outward or homeward bound, when the long journey was ended and the ship had reached port, a life of a very different kind commenced for the foremast hands, as soon as the day's work was done and if not prohibited by quarantine or the captain: everybody, down to the lowly cabin boy, became an individual once again, with money jingling in their pockets at that. Dressed decently, they could at last go where they pleased and do whatever their hearts desired—singly, in pairs or groups formed by similarity of age or country of origin. In port, ashore, the human being with his different needs came into his rights again: the body with its appetites, thirst for stimulants and oblivion, sexual desire—to be sure; but also the mind and the spirit. Many sailors visited museums and churches, attended lectures and Labor Union assemblies in whatever part of the world they might be finding themselves. Between times they could eat and drink, what and where they liked, with nobody to interfere with their freedom, nobody to "boss them around". Shore life, seen from the outside, seemed to be freer from harassment than life on board. Replete and content, the tars were free to "launch themselves" for an evening cruise: visit the Hippodrome, go and hear a Ladies' Band, show their prowess in feats of strength. In the evening, the crew would re-assemble—loudly and cheerfully singing—at the sailor's boarding house—or else in the "Kallabus" (calaboose), say at Iquique, or the David Street police lock-up in Hamburg.

Tattooing parlors were much the vogue; from the sample book of the skin-prick artist the sailors chose their personal ornaments. In the second half of the 18th century, the passion for having themselves painfully but decoratively skin-pricked had become universal with the European sailors almost overnight, evidently an outgrowth of the British and French voyages of discovery to the South Sea, especially to Tahiti.

In the Sailors' Village

Villages of central and northern Europe principally inhabited by a seagoing population, whether situated on the coast or inland, showed in the 18th and 19th centuries many differences, even in external appearance, from agricultural settlements of approximately the same number of inhabitants, even if they were close neighbors. In the maritime settlement the manor house or local nobleman's chateau would be lacking; in its place, there would more likely be a village schoolhouse, even before the epoch of compulsory universal education. Instead of the village green and church, the harbor was the focal point in the sailors' village. In some sheltered nook in sight of the quays, a group of benches were the headquarters for the local old gentlemen with their seafaring days behind them. It was their lookout and communications center. Shops in the village streets had signs proclaiming colonial goods or ships' supplies. Instead of the "Schützenhaus" or "The Bear" you would find the "Skippers' Exchange" or "The Anchor" as names for inns and taverns. On the counter of the bar in the taproom, the boat-shaped collection box for the victims of the sea was never missing. The churches also were marked by the maritime life: steeples had ships as weather vanes; inside, numerous donations made by seamen, and inscribed as such by the donors, were to be seen: window-panes with ship paintings, altar candelabra and chandeliers, Eucharistic vessels, commemorative tablets, and almost invariably one or several ship models. In the cemetery, the tombstones with reliefs of ships caught the eye; the neat and well cared-for corner reserved for the nameless dead washed ashore was another striking feature (ill. 140). In the maritime villages one also found linguistic peculiarities, e.g. the frequent conjunction of a family name with a ship's name, for purposes of identification, such as Cito-Lewe, Marie-Voss, etc. Geographical and nautical directions were much used: the north end of the village, the west side of a house, to windward of the forest.

A sailor's homestead unmistakably proclaimed itself as such from the outside. Amid the flower beds of the front yard a flagpole with a weather vane on top; a dismounted old deckhouse or a rowboat, sawn in half and stood up on end, as tool shed, were sure signs. In the old whaling communities, garden gates flanked by the gigantic jawbones of whales were often seen. The use of ships' name-boards and retired riding lights above house entrances was common. Where the disposition of the shore permitted, every sailor's house had its own boat landing.

Design and construction of the houses, were generally in the style of the region, but the shipmasters were the first to have their houses built in urban fashion.

Left: *140 Grave of blubber flenser Ocke Hagen (1752–1841)
on the North Friesian island of Föhr, who sailed for many decades
in Dutch whaling vessels (after Wanda Oesau).*

*141 E. Laschke: Barkentine "Mönchgut" of Thiessow on Rügen.
Oil painting, painted 1877 at North Shields.*
*In the eyes of shipmasters in all European seamen's villages and
seaport towns, a portrait of the vessel commanded by them was the
most general emblem of civic standing by the middle of the
18th century. In such a picture everything was of equal importance: the
inscription at the bottom, almost invariably a part of the composition,*
proclaiming the type and name of the vessel and her home-port, no
less than a fitting background: Kronborg Castle, Heligoland,
Gibraltar, Naples with Vesuvius, etc. Originally paintings of this
genre had been made by laymen, that is to say by sailors who knew
their subject matter better than the art of perspective; they created
pictures of naive accuracy. A root of this maritime folk art lies in the
votive tablet paintings of the Mediterranean region. Some of the
specialties that developed during the flourishing of ship-painting
were the portraits of European vessels made on commission by Chinese
and Japanese artists; also the paintings behind glass from the
19th century, made in Ostende and Antwerp.

142 *On Shrove Tuesday the Baltic sailors celebrated their traditional*
festival. During the morning they paraded through the streets with
a large ship model. Later in the day there was a banquet and in the
evening, the sailors' ball. Our picture was taken around 1880 in
Nakskov in Denmark.

143 *Ancient Mesopotamian toy boat from a child's grave in Warka,*
about 7th century B. C.

144 Children of the Uro, a fishing population inhabiting islands in Lake Titicaca, playing with rafts made of bundles of rushes.

145 *Raft made by children of bundles of sedges. Ückermünde on the Oderhaff, 1972*

*146 Russian "Pomor" boats in the harbor of Hammerfest in northern
Norway, about 1890. "Pomor trade" was the name given in the
fjord region of Finnmark to the traditional barter of fish for agricultural produce, between the Norwegian Lapp fishermen and Russian merchant sailors.*

147 *Cecil Trew: Lakatoi from New Guinea. Drawing, 1936.*
The lakatoi of the southeast coast of New Guinea were composed of
several dugout canoes connected by cross beams supporting a stable
deck, on which there was room for a shelter for the crew and the
cargo, and on which the two masts were erected. Every year at the
season of the autumn monsoon the Papuan Motu sailors departed on
extensive trading voyages with whole squadrons of these vessels. The
lakatoi were laden with ceramic goods, which the traders exchanged
for sago and logs for canoe-building. Similar bartering relations
(kula) were described by Bronislaw Malinowski in his book "Argonauts
of the Western Pacific" (1922). The Massim-Melanesians living on the
numerous islets off the southeast coast of New Guinea also undertook
extensive annual round trips by boat during the spring monsoon,
bartering bracelets, shell necklaces, ceramic wares and big stone
hatchets—objects more of a ritual value than of economical useful-
ness. All kula activities were carried out on the beach only, and ex-
clusively among men, following a strictly observed ritual. Every
trading partner had to respond to the gift made to him with a
counter-gift of like value. The more trading partners a man could
prove to have had dealings with, the greater became his public
stature. The bartered objects had to be re-traded continually. The
boats used exclusively for kula travels were lavishly ornamented and
individualized by being given names. They were built jointly by all
the villagers and were community property.

148 *Venetian gondola, the traditional boat for passenger traffic of the lagoon city of the Adriatic Sea. They are rowed from a standing position.*

Right:
149 *In many parts of the world water craft of all kinds play an important role in the distribution of consumer goods, whether for transporting merchandise and customers to the market place, or in trading from ship to ship in harbor. This was still common practice in Europe on rivers, creeks and canals two or three decades ago. In the seaports, ship victuallers operated their "bumboats". In some cities floating markets have become famous. Bangkok has a boat market on the klongs (canals) at the west shore of the Menam, a small section of which is shown in our illustration.*

Left: *150 Zeesboot from the bays between the island of Rügen and the Darss, used for non-motorized trawling for eel and zander. With the square-rigged dragnet boats of the Zalew Wislany (lagoon of the Vistula) they constitute the last sailing vessels in the Baltic fisheries.*

151 Arab dhow. These vessels are carvel-built with sewn plank seams; they are excellent monsoon sailers and today still negotiate the major part of the non-European marine trade between the Persian Gulf and the Suaheli coast of East Africa.

152 The Kotoko fishers from the Shari delta and the southwest shore of Lake Chad make their boats of planks sewn together. As this bow shows, the single parts are first basted in order to bring them in the right position.

153 Sewn bottom-plank boat, between 10 and 15 meters long (markaba) of the Kotoko fishing population.

Right:
154 Rafts made of bundles of papyrus (kadai) of the Buduma-Yidena, the population of the 100 or so islands in Lake Chad.
The fishermen caste of this tribe is widely known for its excellent craftmanship in building rafts and net-making, while the fisher women make pottery and weave textiles; the women also participate in ritual ceremonies. The upper castes of the Buduma engage exclusively in cattle raising, and enriched themselves further in the old times by slave trading and cattle stealing. Possibly the low caste of the fishermen, who are regarded as unclean, descended from older hunting tribes, subjugated at some earlier period by the cattle breeders. The kadais are propelled by poling in the shallow waters of the lake. They can load up to 6 tons of cargo and are always fitted with cooking hearths. In these vessels the Buduma undertake trips lasting a week or more.

155 Boat landing on the Indian coast.
Beach settlements like the one illustrated are often not permanently
inhabited, but have a seasonally changing population. Depending on
weather conditions, which are determined by the monsoons, and on
the seasonal fishing patterns, the fishermen wander along the coast
from one place to another and back again, as described by Alfred
Radcliffe-Brown for the Andamanese, and by Frederick Rose for the
northern Australian aboriginal population of Groote Eylandt. This
nomadic phenomenon may be today observed in its purest form in
West Africa, where the Fanti fishermen follow the schools of sar-
dines, and migrate in the course of the year the entire length of the
Guinea coast from Senegal to the Niger, disregarding national
boundaries, and returning only in the inclement season to their
ancestral pile dwellings.

156 Dugout with outboard motor in a pile settlement in Venezuela
(Lake Maracaibo).

In the Caribbean, on the banks of the Orinoco and Amazon, on the
West African Guinea coast and the Congo, as well as everywhere in
Southeast Asia, there are pile-dwelling settlements. Essential to every
household are rafts or boats. The pile-dwellers must have them in
order to be able to go fishing and to market, to the village bar
(complete with television set), to the mission dispensary, school and
church.

Boats are also indispensable for the erection of new pile dwellings. At
the building site, the piles are lowered vertically into the water, until
firm bottom has been reached through the thick layer of mud. A man
then seizes the pile and hangs from it with all his weight, leaving
his feet in the boat, which is moved rapidly ahead and astern by
two paddlers. Through this forward and backward motion a hole is
made in the mud, water penetrating into it at once. The pile is
sucked firmly into the mud. In this manner the big uprights can be
planted without much difficulty.

A study was made recently of the fishing villages composed of
260 pile structures of the Paraujano Indians on the lagoons of Lake
Maracaibo in Venezuela, in order to ascertain what cultural changes
have occurred. Despite considerable modern influences, essential elements of the traditional culture have been maintained: the houses,
equipment for transportation and most of the fishing gear, and the
vitally important log canoes. These are made in the lagoon in the
same unchanged technique of centuries ago. Some of the canoes have
outboard motors, however, and there are some specialists who know
how to repair such engines.

Left: 157 Tanka boat dwelling near Hongkong.
Roughly 100,000 people live aboard vessels in the Hongkong area.
Perhaps half that number are ocean or freshwater fishermen and
pearl divers. None know any other homes and have no property on
shore. The total number of the boat-dwelling Tanka population of the
southern Chinese provinces of Kwantung, Kwangsi and Fukien, which
has been traced back to the medieval Sung period of the 9th–13th
centuries, is estimated to be about a million. The inhabitants of these
floating villages, which are well administered on a partnership basis,
are not nomadic, even though some of the fishing groups have a
certain seasonal mobility of their own. In their dialect, folklore,
social organization and characteristic customs they are quite distinct
from the peasant population of the adjacent land. In earlier times the
Tanka were a low-caste coastal population, excluded from crafts,
trade and public education.
Similar groups lived in South Korea and Japan (Ama, Noji). Prob-
ably they were remnants of an archaic fishing population forced into
the status of pariah and isolated in their boat villages by foreign
ruling classes in the early phase of expanding feudalism.

158 Floating houses in Vietnam. From: Globus 58/1890.
In three principal regions in the world rafts are used as supports for
permanent dwellings: in Southeast Asia, on the Amazon and the
Congo. In the Amazon town of Manaus, famous around the turn of
the century during the period of caoutchouc production, hundreds of
raft dwellings, moored to piles and interconnected with gangplanks,
form a floating fishermen's suburb, harboring all essential shops as
well as many seafood restaurants, where among other delicacies the
pirarucu (arapaima gigas), the biggest freshwater fish in the world,
is served. The coupled bamboo rafts, which may be many hundred
meters long, of the floating villages of South China, Indochina and
Malaya, even bear sizeable gardens which are carefully cultivated.

159 *Junk sailmaker in the harbor of Tsingtao.*

Right:
160 *Compared with modern sailing yachts, aptly characterized by professionals as "racing machines", the hulls and rigs of yachts from the turn of the century were of considerably greater aesthetic appeal. This photograph shows the British cutter "Créole", built in 1890, racing at Cowes in 1913 (Beken).*

161 Danish cutter fisherman at his radio transmitter.

In North Germany this meant that they would front on the street, not presenting a gable end. Confortableness was more important than economic viewpoints. The interior plan was in the town style, with a special dining-room used only for festivities in wintertime. Furniture, once part of the ship's inventory, and nautical souvenirs were in every room, beginning with the entrance, where the sea chests stood and the great ship's barometer hung. The living room was often furnished with imported pieces down to the last item, among which would be sofa, rocking chair, a stand for potted flowers, writing desk, mirror console, wall clock and hanging lamp. Much in favor were wall panellings of Dutch tiles with ship pictures; also tiled stoves decorated with Swedish ceramics showing marine subjects.

The clothes closets harbored long Scottish shawls, silken wraps, suits made of English cloth. The dish cupboards were filled with silverware, Chinese porcelain, English stoneware. In the kitchen there was hardly a utensil for everyday use that had not come from England—not to mention the provisions of coffee, tea, spices, wine, rum, whiskey or gin. In the apartment of the elders were to be seen the nautical instruments that had come ashore with retirement: barometer, sextant, chronometer, astronomical tables, nautical almanac. In every skipper's dwelling the portrait of the ship the "Old Man" had commanded was hung, in watercolor or oils, with a broad gold frame (ill.141). And even in the more frugally furnished habitations of simple sailors, the visitor would be shown souvenirs of blue-water voyages: curios such as tropical sea shells, coconuts, stuffed sea birds or flying fish, a Chinese fan, some Eskimo carving, a copper-glaze golden pot or the inevitable pair of Staffordshire dogs.

Another very striking feature of the sailors' village were the largely deserted streets during the cruising season, March through December. During these months one saw only women, children, and a few elders abroad—and the children only in bad weather. The men returned home only after the beginning of the northern winter forced a cessation of coastwise navigation. The weeks following their homecoming were full of activity, despite the rigors of the climate. Necessary repairs were made to the houses. The men went in groups into the woods, to get the winter's supply of firewood; they also went eel-spearing on the ice near the beach. Some worked as boatbuilders, sledge-makers, basket weavers or broom-makers. The weddings that had been arranged during the year were celebrated after copious preparations.

The ships' captains settled with their fellow share-holders for gains or losses incurred by the ships during the past season. Partnership owning of vessels, with graduated

162 Silken banner of the Sailors' Guild of Sonderburg in Schleswig, 1614. The scene combines a representation of a large ship of the period with the biblical motif of the prophet Jonah being cast overboard (after J. Raben).

shares of up to 1/64th part of the original building cost, had begun as an institution of the feudal sea cities, and after 1650 the coastal villages adopted the system.

Amalgamated with the traditional community spirit of village society and mutual assistance among neighbors, partnership navigation became the economic and ideological basis of early rural capitalist sea trade in northern Europe. Similarly on the basis of mutual assistance, skippers founded shipbuilding credit and insurance associations, the annual meetings of which were held in the time between the New Year and Shrove Tuesday. On Hiddensee and in some other villages there was also a partnership company to operate a regular steamer connection. After the model of the seamen's guilds and fraternities, which had existed in all the seaports since the Middle Ages—and

one at least still exists today in an active role: the Stralsund Shipmasters' Company, founded 1488—the village people organized in the 18th and 19th centuries shipmasters' and sailors' associations with the purpose of cultivating sociable contact among families during the winter months, and also, in conjunction with an aid society for the widows and orphans of seamen, to provide a social welfare service.

During the carnival all these associations staged their various banquets and balls, part of which celebration was a parade through the village, a decorated ship model often forming part of the pageant (ill. 142). Such customs have their origin in the towns and cities of the lower Rhine and Schelde as far back as the 12th century. In later times artistic representations of ships assumed the same character of traditional symbols in the villages which they had earlier in the cities. Individuals as well as companies used the ship image as a symbol of civic class-consciousness, the former in their ship portraits, the latter in various ways: ship models in the churches, which in the 18th century still served as public meeting places of fishermen and sailors; emblems on the banners of the seamen's associations, on business signs and stationery, and on the house flags of the partnership companies (ill, 162).

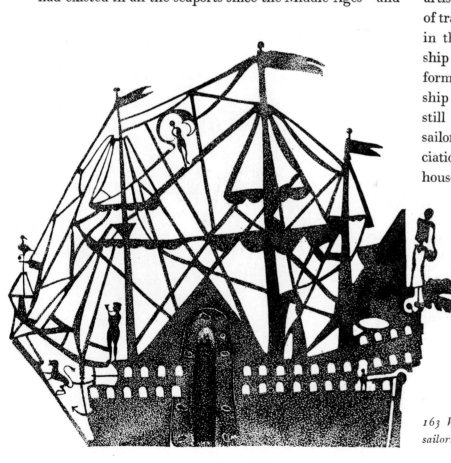

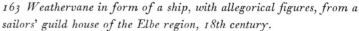

163 Weathervane in form of a ship, with allegorical figures, from a sailors' guild house of the Elbe region, 18th century.

As soon as he is able to get to the beach, a sailor's son or fisher boy wants a toy boat, by preference something he can make for himself, out of driftwood, some twigs and a rag of cloth for a sail. His toy boat not only teaches him to observe wind, current and the tides, but by playing with it he learns about the rigging and how to make knots (ill. 143).

As he gets bolder he ventures into making a raft for himself out of bundles of reeds or sedges, or some beams laid cross-wise, and he sets out on a trip along the shore, poling his craft in the shallow water (ill. 144, 145). If a father is able to bring the proper understanding to this momentous turning point, he turns over a real boat to his youngster. Now he can and will learn how to row, scull, sail and steer, and all this is not just play, either. Most boys want to make themselves useful at home, and most of all those whose fathers are away at sea during three quarters of the year. In a fatherless household they want to move into the position of masculine responsibilities: they insist on rowing the boat for their mother when she is going to the store, the pasture or the steamer landing; they set fish traps, so they can provide for the dinner table. They splice the clothes line, gather gulls' eggs, driftwood, clam shells and seaweed for the garden; for grandmother, they pick bouquets of water lilies and spatterdock. In all these things they copy their fathers; they wear dad's cap and clogs, use the professional jargon and try to brag as they hear their elders do, including the oaths—they are growing into the role of the seafarer.

164 Boys from Somalia playing with self-made model boats (after Vinigi Grottanelli).

The Fish Market

The traditional bartering of fish for flour, groats, butter and cheese, also for lumber and birch bark, which was carried on during the 18th and 19th centuries between Norwegian and Lapp fishermen on the one side, and Russian skippers on the other, was called the "Pomor" trade in the northern Scandinavian coastal regions. "Pomorje" (on the sea) was the Russian name for the Russian White Sea coast about Archangel. Some 2000 boats were annually active in the Pomor trade from June through September. The trading from ship to ship was regulated by set customs; for example, the testing of the fish and flour samples and the weighing of the goods was done under the supervision of the Fisher Elder. In the course of time a special Pomor trade language came into being on this coast, which both sides could understand. We can visualize the dimensions of this shipping trade when we learn that, of a Sunday, the little town of Hammerfest, of some 3,500 inhabitants, played host to some 6000–7000 "Boat Russians"! (ill.146).

A quite similar and regular barter trade was in use until the beginning of this century between the Finnish and Estonian coastal population inhabiting the shores of the Gulf of Finland. Twice a year, in late June and late September, the Finnish island fishermen brought their salted small herrings to barter for corn and potatoes with the Estonians. An ancient agreement had established that one measure of fish should equal two measures of rye grain. Peasants and fishermen formed fixed barter relations, called "friends" in Estonian, among whom the trading went on along the accustomed lines for generation after generation. The trading was opened by the Finns offering their respective "friends" a meal of fried fish, served on tree bark platters, and treating the peasants to coffee and schnapps. The Finnish wives brought aprons to give as presents to the Estonian women. On their side, the peasants treated with eggs, cabbage and home-brewed beer. These market days on the beach were like feast days: there was trading, drinking and dancing. In this area too, a mixed Finnish-Estonian language was used for communication.

Of lesser scope, but showing a strict observance of similar customs, were other exchange agreements elsewhere in the Baltic area, between those families whose livelihood was entirely derived from fishing, aquatic game and beach gathering, without agriculture or cattle raising, and the peasants on the adjacent land tracts. These fishermen exploited to the fullest possible extent all opportunities for extracting food and raw materials from "the beach". As recently as the early part of this century, they captured seals, sea otters and sea birds, besides fish. Their wives and children harvested gulls' eggs, crayfish, clams, snails, aquatic plants, berries, herbs, mushrooms and nuts. Birds' feathers, otter skins, train oil made from seals, and seaweed were used in the households. Clam shells, snails and small fry were used, together with roots of water-lilies and water aloe, for domestic animal feed. Algae were gathered for garden fertilizer, reeds for cattle bedding, bulrushes for roofing. Besides wood, the fishers used stones from the beach, bones and the stalks of water plants as raw materials for making their tools and equipment. Anything else that might be wanted in the way of consumer goods or raw material had to be acquired by barter.

Every fisherman on the coast of the Skagerrak had his traditional place for bartering dried, salt or fresh fish against corn, meat and potatoes. In the autumn, the fisher women sailed or rowed to the meeting place, singly or in groups of as many as ten to twenty boats, while the peasant women journeyed to the rocky islands with milk, butter, cheese and fruit. Every year the Swedish fishermen from the islands of the Uppland province sailed with their cargo of salt herrings into the remotest corners of the Lake Mälar region, a good 200 kilometers. On these trips they lived for weeks and months in their open boats. At night a tent of oars and sails was rigged in the vessel (ill.165). The cooking was done on an open hearth in the after part of the boat. This tenting in boats was a customary feature of living, especially for those fishermen who made annual seasonal trips to often very remote seasonal fishing grounds, the *Vitte*, *Bude* or *fiskerlejer*. With Swedes and Finns it was the custom for the men only to make the trip, six to eight weeks in the spring and again in the late summer; with Livs and Courlanders, the whole village population migrated, six to eight months, "from ice to ice", living in a summer camp formed by the beached boats.

Four different nationalities came in contact on the eastern Baltic coast during these bartering expeditions: Livs, Courlanders, Lithuanians and Germans. But also within the home country of each nation, the regular, at least bi-weekly, trips to the more local fish market mediated a lively cultural exchange between the fishing villages and the urban way of living. It was through this interchange that urban middle-class ways of building and furnishing houses, ideas of nutrition, etc. gradually made their way into these remote regions; likewise, innovations such as the cultivation of orchards and vegetable farms or the establishment of extensive dairy farming were introduced to the fisher settlements of the southern Baltic which, growing out of early feudal colonies of serfs, originally knew neither agriculture nor cattle breeding.

165 Fishing boat with tent dwelling moored in the Stockholm Fish Market (from a view of the city from the middle of the 19th century).

The Transformation of Coastal Trade and Fishing Ports

During the past few years we all have observed far-reaching structural changes in the port activities of the coastal area of the North Sea and the Baltic. Pipelines, barge operation, both motorized and pushed, containerized transport and the through-traffic of ferried trailer trucks have revolutionized the metropolitan industrial ports, while the changes produced by progressive urbanization and the growth of the tourist trade affect chiefly the harbors of small towns and of the many villages of the region. Among these we also count the numerous rural wharves and landing places handling the produce of large farms and factories, which sprang up around the turn of the century; likewise, the small fishing ports, boat and steamer landings and winter quarters for the sailing coasters of village navigation, protected or created by packed stone breakwaters or moles; lastly the open loading places for lumber, sand and seaweed on the beach and without any artificial protective structures.

Installations of this description were exceedingly numerous at the outset of the 20th century in the North Sea and Baltic area. For example no fewer than 52 harbors were counted in the year 1935 on the island of Rügen alone. At the same period there were in the Kleine Oderhaff (lesser Oder lagoon) 16 fishing boat harbors and 8 loading stations for brickworks besides the urban harbors of Usedom and Ückermünde. These places had their own characteristics. Part of the picture were the venerable harbormaster, the buxom fisher women in their quayside stalls, the yard master of the railroad with his whistle, the old-timers come to an anchor on the *Klöhnbank* (gossip bench). Wooden quays, reedy shores, corn silos, boatyards, harborside inns, ship chandlers' stores, sail lofts and blacksmiths' shops completed the scene. Here was the place to see the local steamer, horse-drawn trucks and wagons, fishermen's sheds, frames for drying nets, tar tubs, anchors, mooring bitts and what not. Add the sounds—the busy bell and whistle of the steam switching locomotive of the harbor branch of the railroad, the early rumbling of dozens of blow torches starting the hot-bulb motors of the boats—and the indescribable harbor aroma compounded of tar, oak shavings, smoked sprats, the green cloak of algae on the mooring piles, of mud and decaying seaweed. These are the elements that come to mind when evoking the small-craft and fishing harbor in northern Europe of the past.

From the 1930s on, and at an increased rate after the end of the Second World War, all countries in northern Europe underwent the far-reaching political, economic and cultural changes with which we are familiar; changes affecting all of society in terms of industrialization and continued urbanization, while the lives of individuals are modified chiefly through motor tourism and other leisure time activities. The village ports and their life rhythm did not escape this wave of change. The open loading places and primitive wintering harbors of rustic shipping have disappeared entirely. The picture of the village harbor such as we have tried to describe it is totally transmuted today: we see refrigeration sheds, canned-goods factories, oil storage tanks and modern repair shops. What was formerly a factory port, located well into the country, away from habitations, has become a supply dock for a nuclear power plant. A novelty on the scene is the marina, the aquatic sports center used by sailing and canoeing enthusiasts, skin divers, motor tourists and sport fishermen.

Some of the skills that, less than a century ago, were an essential part of the traditional working world, can be counted, where they subsist in our generation, only under the heading of sport and play, as leisure activities. This applies to non-mechanized fishing and sailing. Nevertheless, points of contact between old-time professional sailors' work and water sports still exist. The yachtsman may choose an old fishing cutter or small coaster for his wanderings, instead of a standardized, one-design vessel of mass production. The seaman today may employ his vacation or other leisure time in sailing, canoeing or fishing peacefully from some beach or reedy shore. Professional and amateur alike share a revival of interest in traditionally rigged vessels and in meeting the challenge of wind and sea. According to a recent news item, more than a quarter of a million sport boats were counted in Scandinavia, distributed among 16 million inhabitants. This gives an idea of the extent to which water sports have grown in our time. The U.S.A. is still leading in this type of recreation, but Europeans are coming close with tens of thousands of canoeing enthusiasts, oarsmen and sailing addicts on rivers, lakes and on the coast.

Sport sailing had its origin in the Netherlands, where since the 17th century the wealthy and influential bourgeois patricians amused themselves with their "pleasure yachts". From the Low Countries yachting spread, through the medium of the royal courts, to England, France, Prussia, Russia and Scandinavia. Around the middle of the last century the competitive voyages of the clippers inspired American yachtsmen to a first try at a transatlantic race in 1866; since that year many a rugged sailing contest has been waged on the Atlantic and elsewhere. In 1908 sailing became one of the disciplines in the Olympic Games.

The yacht clubs which all the major cities of northern Europe founded in the period between 1830 and 1840 preserved for the most part an attitude of aristocratic snobbery and exclusiveness well into modern times. In contrast thereto, a radical novelty was represented by the founding of the *Arbeitersegelverein* (working men's sailing association) "Fraternitas" in 1891 at Berlin.

Henceforth, sailing enthusiasts of modest means and working classes had gained access to this type of recreation. In this period the first steps toward a popular sport were taken, to which a considerable contributing factor was canoe camping. Coming from England, the U.S.A. and Sweden, this sport had become very popular toward the end of the century. In 1905 the first Foldboat had been tried out in southern Germany; after the First World War, this type of water wandering greatly helped to broaden the water sports scene. Motor boating had begun to be a form of pleasure boating shortly following the turn of the century; steam yachting, which had especially flourished in England, may be seen as a precursor. The building and racing of model yachts probably belongs somewhere halfway between play and sport. The first regatta of model yachts was sailed at London in 1853; as early as 1908 radio steering control for model sailing yachts had been successfully tried out.

Shall we try a feuilletonistic sketch of the new picture of today's small harbor? The harbormaster in our seaside village is called "Captain" and wears a uniform with gold braid. The deckhands of the fishing cutters arrive at their work on heavy motorcycles; the shipowner, when ready to depart, hoists his car aboard, which had been parked alongside his coastal freighter during loading. The yardmen of the railroad have walky-talkies; fish is purchased from slender, professional female sales personnel in clinical white. The sailmaker fists featherweight synthetic fabrics. The youthful master carpenter of the boatyard is taking a course in welding and experiments with the fabrication of plastic hulls. The men who have been around the Horn have been dead a long time.

The quays of our new harbors are made of steel and concrete and have electric outlets, running water and telephone connections. The modern village harbor scene is incomplete without filling stations, waterside parking lots, sales and service stations for outboard motors, sporting goods stores, rental agencies for inflatable rafts and portable TV sets, not to forget ice-cream shops, beer gardens, cake and hot dog stands and light beach literature for sale everywhere; lastly, bungalows and tent areas wherever the eye alights. New in the picture are flippered skin divers with their back-pack breathing tanks, and the water-ski maniacs rushing around behind roaring motor boats. The chain-dangling riders of the merry-go-round are old and familiar, but regattas, cruising rallies and sport fishing tournaments are new. The quayside taverns have disappeared—*Gemütlichkeit* has been banished from the harbor area.

Where are the fleets of small vessels? What became of the sloops, smacks, tjalks, three-masted spritsail barges and galiots, the tugboats and passenger steamers, the schooners with stovepipe exhausts from the hot-bulb motors as high as a man? Many of them have been dumped in out-of-the-way places, machinery decaying in the rushes on the beach, except where the authorities have insisted on their removal because of the deplorable pollution of the environment. Some few old-time vessels have been reclaimed and are used as dwellings, a few preserving their former style, others wretchedly disfigured.

A very few old working vessels have ended up as museums. A fine example of conservation was set by the Zuiderzee-Museum in Enkhuizen (founded in 1948) which was the first nautical museum to depart from the established pattern of preserving some veteran of deep-water voyages, choosing instead no fewer than 25 vessels of the Dutch fishing and coastal types. The Norwegian Marine Museum at Bygdøy near Oslo followed suit, when it exhibited the most important boats of its collection of 50 indigenous vessels in a special hall completed in 1958. Other museums to join in this movement were the Berlin Ethnological

Museum and the Oceanographic Museum in Stralsund, whose collection also contains old marine engines. Out of the ordinary was the decision of the Danish National Museum to purchase the fore-and-aft schooner "Fulton"—a vessel belonging to a type characteristic of the extinct coastal navigation of Baltic and North Sea. This vessel was commissioned in 1970; it is used for special courses, excursions and ethnographical research expeditions (ill. p.221).

However, wooden vessels moved only by sail or oar are far from extinct in the world as yet. From the Atlantic coast of Ireland to the Zuiderzee and the Halligen (exposed islets off the coast) of Schleswig, from the Norwegian Finnmark fjords to the Skärgard (archipelago of small, rocky islets) of Stockholm, from the Schlei River in Holstein to the Oderhaff lagoon, simple boats still function: vessels not designed on drawing boards nor mass produced in series of hundreds, they suffice to the needs of a marine working sphere not yet totally urbanized and industrialized. Children still ride their reed-rafts today, still play at floating their toy dugouts and bark shell boats. One-man boats are in use in our time as they were untold ages ago; there are still partnership companies of seafarers in the world; skippers' wives live their workaday lives aboard; boatbuilders and sailmakers still work with adze and marlinspike. Not that the ship folk have refused to go with the times: nowadays the master of a fishing cutter handles his two-way radio and other electronic equipment with the same matter-of-fact ease as his grandfather, in his day, got the hang of his first hot-bulb motor (ill.161). Dutch and Scandinavian sailors' wives are able to steer their three-hundred-ton craft by Decca and radar if necessary. Tradition and progress are held in the same hand, and are sailing board to board on the same course.

Right: The three-masted fore-and-aft schooner "Fulton"
of the Danish National Museum in Copenhagen.

Bibliography
Glossary of Technical Terms
Index
Picture Sources

Bibliography

Adney, Edwin Tappan & Howard Irwing Chapelle, *The bark canoes and skin boats of North America*. Washington 1964

Aijmer, Göran, *The Dragon Boat Festival in Hunan and Hupeh, China*. Stockholm 1964

Åkerlund, Harald, *Fartygsfynden i den forna hamnen i Kalmar*. Stockholm 1951

Anderson, Eugene N., *The boat people of South China*. Anthropos 65 (1970)

Arima, Eugene, *Report on an Eskimo umiak built in 1960*. Ottawa 1963

Audemard, Louis, *Les jonques chinoises*. Rotterdam 1957–1970

Baker, William, *From paddle-steamer to nuclear ship*. London 1965

Bass, George F., *Cape Gelidonia – A bronze age shipwreck*. Transactions of the American Philosophical Society, NS 57 (1967)

Bassett, Fletcher S., *Legends and superstitions of the sea and of sailors*. Chicago/New York 1885

Bénoit, Fernand, *L'épave du Grand Congloué à Marseille*. Paris 1961

Beylen, Jules van, *Vlaamse maritieme achterglasschilderijen*. Mededelingen Marine Academie van Belgie 11 (1958/59)

–, *Zeeuwse visschersschepen van de Ooster- en Westerschelde*. Amsterdam 1963

–, *De versiering van jachten, binnenschepen en vissersvaartuigen in de Nederlanden*. Neerlands Volksleven 13 (1963)

–, *Repertory of Maritime Museums and collections*. Antwerp 1969

Bock, René de & Maurice Seghers, *Binnenvaartuigen en visschersschepen op de Schelde*. Antwerp 1942

–, *De laatste visschersschepen van de vlaamsche kust*. Antwerp 1943

Brøgger, Anton Wilhelm & Haakon Shetelig, *Osebergfundet*. Christiania 1917

Buck, Peter Henry, *Vikings of the sunrise*. New York 1938

Bugge, Anders, *Golden vanes of Viking ships*. Acta archaeologica 2 (1931)

Casson, Lionel, *Ships and Seamanship in the Ancient World*. Princeton N. J. 1971

Cederlund, Carl Olof, *Om hamnväsendets förändringar*. Unda maris 28 (1969/70)

Chapelle, Howard Irwing, *The history of American sailing ships*. New York 1935

–, *American small sailing craft*. New York 1951

Clason, Edward & Anders Franzén, *Wasa – fynd och bärgning*. Stockholm 1959

Crone, Ernst, *Nederlandsche jachten, binnenschepen, visschersvaartuigen 1650–1900*. Amsterdam 1926

Crumlin-Pedersen, Ole, *Skonnerten "Fulton" af Marstal*. Roskilde 1970

Donnelly, Ivan Arthur, *Chinese junks*. Shanghai 1924

Edwards, Clinton, *Aboriginal watercraft on the Pacific coast of South America*. Berkeley and Los Angeles 1965

Ellmers, Detlef, *Keltischer Schiffbau*. Jahrbuch Römisch-germanisches Nationalmuseum Mainz 16 (1969)

Erixon, Sigurd, *Kirchenbootgemeinschaften. Technik und Gemeinschaftsbildungen*. Stockholm 1957

Eskeröd, Albert, *Båtar från ekstock till trålare*. Stockholm 1970

Firth, Raymond, *Malay fishermen*. London 1946

Fliedner, Siegfried & Rosemarie Pohl-Weber, *Die Bremer Hanse-Kogge. Fund, Konservierung, Forschung*. Bremen 1969

Fonseca, Quirino da, *A caravela portuguesa*. Coimbra 1934

Fraser, Thomas M., *Rusembilan – A Malay fishing village*. Ithaca N. Y. 1960

Friederici, Georg, *Die Schiffahrt der Indianer*. Stuttgart 1907

Frobenius, Leo, *Der Kameruner Schiffsschnabel und seine Motive*. Halle 1897

Gerndt, Helge, *Fliegender Holländer und Klabautermann*. Göttingen 1971

Golson, Jack, *Polynesian navigation*. Wellington N. Z. 1963

Greenhill, Basil, *The merchant schooners*. Newton Abbot 1968, 2nd ed.

–, *Boats and boatmen of Pakistan*. Newton Abbot 1971

Grinsell, L. V., *The boat of the dead in the Bronze Age*. Antiquity 15 (1941)

Grottanelli, Vinigi, *Pescatori dell'Oceano Indiano*. Rome 1955

Gusinde, Martin, *Die Feuerland-Indianer*. Vol. 2. Die Yamana. Mödling 1937

Haddon, Alfred Cort & James Hornell, *Canoes of Oceania*. Honolulu 1936–1938

Hagedorn, Bernhard, *Die Entwicklung der wichtigsten Schiffstypen*. Berlin 1914

Hansen, Hans Jürgen, *Kunstgeschichte der Seefahrt*. Oldenburg/Hamburg 1966

Hasslöf, Olof, *Svenska västkustfiskarna*. Göteborg 1949

Hasslöf, Olof & Henning Henningsen & Arne Emil Christensen jun., *Sømand, fisker, skib og værft. Introduction til maritim etnologi*. Copenhagen 1970

Heims, Paul Gerhard, *Seespuk. Aberglaube, Märchen und Schnurren*. Leipzig 1888

Henningsen, Henning, *Kirkeskibe og kirkeskibsfester*. Copenhagen 1950

–, *Bådeoptog in Danske søkøbstaeder*. Copenhagen 1953

–, *Crossing the Equator*. Copenhagen 1961

Henningsen, Henning, *Jonas – Profet og ulykkesfugl.* Årbog Handels- og Søfartsmuseet Kronborg 25 (1966)

–, *Maritime kuriosa og suvenirs.* Årbog Handels- og Søfartsmuseet Kronborg 27 (1968)

Hornell, James, *Survivals of the use of oculi in modern boats.* Journal Royal Anthropological Institute 53 (1923)

–, *British coracles. The curraghs of Ireland.* Mariner's Mirror 22–24 (1936–1938)

–, *Water transport. Origins and early evolution.* Cambridge 1946

Hourani, George, *Arab seafaring in the Indian Ocean.* Princeton 1951

Hugill, Stan, *Shanties from the seven seas.* London 1961

–, *Sailortown.* London 1967

Itkonen, Toivo Immanuel, *Suomen kansanomaiset veneet.* Suomen Museo 33 (1926)

–, *Suomen ruuhet.* Kansatieteellinen arkisto 5 (1942)

Ivens, Walter George, *The island builders of the Pacific.* London 1930

Kampen, H.C.A. van & H.Kersken, *Schepen die voorbijgaan.* s'Gravenhage 1927

Kano, Tadao & Kokichi Segawa, *The Yami. Illustrated ethnography of Formosa aborigines.* Tokyo 1956, 2nd ed.

Kauffmann, Hans, *Die Nouka auf dem Sangu, ein Bootstyp in Ostpakistan.* Zeitschrift für Ethnologie 94 (1969)

Kemp, Dixon, *A manual of yacht and boat sailing.* London 1878

Kjölsen, Hans H., *Staffordhunde.* Årbog Handels- og Søfartsmuseet Kronborg 28 (1969)

Klausen, Arne Martin, *Kerala fishermen.* Oslo 1968

Klein, Ernst, *De klinkbyggda allmogebåtarna på nordisk område.* Nordisk kultur 16 (1934)

Klem, Knud, *Handels- og Søfartsmuseet 50 år.* Årbog Handels- og Søfartsmuseet Helsingør 24 (1965)

Konrad, Walter, *Die Wasserfahrzeuge der Tschadsee-Region.* Baessler-Archiv, NF 5 (1957)

Köster, August, *Das antike Seewesen.* Berlin 1923

–, *Modelle alter Segelschiffe.* Berlin 1926

Kucharska, Jadwiga, *Tradycyjna organizacja rybolowstwa na wybrzezu Kaszubskim.* Wrocław/Warszawa 1968

Kunze, Walter, *Der Mondseer Einbaum.* Jahrbuch Oberösterreichischer Musealverein 113 (1968)

Lächler, Paul & Hans Wirz, *Die Schiffe der Völker.* Olten/Freiburg 1962

Lage (Die) der in der Seeschiffahrt beschäftigten Arbeiter. Schriften des Vereins für Sozialpolitik Leipzig 103/104 (1903/1904)

Landström, Björn, *Ships of the Pharaos.* New York 1970

Laughton, Leonard Geoffrey Carr, *Old ship figure-heads and stern.* London 1925

Lubbock, Basil, *The log of the "Cutty Sark".* Glasgow 1924

–, *The last of the windjammers.* Vol. 1–2. Glasgow 1927, 1929

–, *The nitrate clippers.* Glasgow 1932

–,, *The opium clippers.* Glasgow 1933

Luts, Arved: *Beziehungen der nordestnischen Küstenbewohner zu Finnland.* Kolloquium Balticum Ethnographicum 1966. Berlin 1968

MacGregor, David R., *The tea clippers.* London 1953

Malinowski, Bronislaw, *Argonauts of the Western Pacific.* London 1922

Manninen, Ilmari, *Zur Ethnologie des Einbaums.* Eurasia Septentrionalis Antiqua 1 (1927)

March, Edgar, J., *Inshore craft of Britain.* Newton Abbot 1970

Marsden, Peter Richard, *A ship of the Roman Period, from Blackfriars in the City of London.* London (1967)

Meissonnier, Jean, *Segelschiffe im Zeitalter der Romantik. Aquarelle und Zeichnungen von Antoine Roux.* Bielefeld 1969

Mitzka, Walther, *Deutsche Bauern- und Fischerboote.* Heidelberg 1933

Molaug, Svein, *Norsk sjøfartsmuseum 1914–1964.* Oslo 1964

Moll, Friedrich, *Das Schiff in der bildenden Kunst.* Bonn 1929

Mookerij, Radha Kumud, *Indian shipping.* London 1912

Müller-Wismar, Wilhelm, *Austroinsulare Kanus als Kult- und Kriegssymbole.* Baessler Archiv 2 (1912)

Müller-Wulckow, Walter, *Das Goldene Schiff von Uelzen. Niederdeutsche Beiträge zur Kunstgeschichte.* Vol. 2. Munich 1962

Neweklowsky, Ernst, *Die Schiffahrt und Flößerei im Raume der oberen Donau.* Vol. 1–3. Linz 1952, 1954, 1964

Nicolaysen, Nikolaus, *Langskibet fra Gokstad ved Sandefjord.* Christiania 1882

Nikkilä, Eino, *En satakundensisk äsping och dess eurasiska motsvarigheter.* Folk-Liv 11 (1947)

Nishimura, Shinji, *Ancient rafts of Japan.* Tokyo 1925

Nooteboom, Christian, *Boomstamkano in Indonesie.* Leiden 1932

–, *Trois problèmes d'ethnologie maritime.* Rotterdam 1952

Oesau, Wanda, *Schleswig-Holsteins Grönlandfahrt auf Walfischfang.* Glückstadt/ Hamburg 1937

224

Olsen, Olaf & Ole Crumlin-Pedersen, *The Skuldelev ships*. Acta archaeologica 38 (1967)

Oman, Charles, *Medieval silver nefs*. London 1963

Paris, Edmond, *Souvenirs de marine*. Vol. 1–4. Paris 1882–1886, 1908

Paris, Pierre, *Esquisse d'une ethnographie navale des peuples Annamites*. Rotterdam 1955

Peesch, Reinhard, *Die Fischerkommünen auf Rügen und Hiddensee*. Berlin 1961

Piétri, J.B., *Voiliers d'Indochine*. Saigon 1943

Prins, Adrian Hendrik Johan, *Sailing from Lamu*. Assen 1965

–, *Islamic maritime magic – A ship's charm from Lamu*. Wort und Religion. Stuttgart 1969

–, *Maritime art in an islamic context – Oculus and therion in Lamu ships*. Mariner's Mirror 56 (1970)

Radcliffe-Brown, Alfred Reginald, *Andaman Islanders*. Cambridge 1922

Reinholdsen, Bernt: *Om pomorhandeln*. By og bygd 21 (Oslo 1968/69)

Rosenberg, Gustav: *Hjortspringfundet*. Copenhagen 1937

Rudolph, Wolfgang: *Die Insel der Schiffer*. Rostock 1962

–, *Handbuch der volkstümlichen Boote im östlichen Niederdeutschland*. Berlin 1966

–, *Segelboote der deutschen Ostseeküste*. Berlin 1969

Schäuffelen, Otmar, *Die letzten großen Segelschiffe*. Bielefeld 1969

Schmidt, Leopold, *Der norische Himmelbootfahrer*. Carinthia I, 141 (1951)

–, *Schifferglaube und Schifferbrauch im Bereich der oberen Donau. Volksglaube und Volksbrauch*. Vienna 1966

Schori, Dieter, *Das Floß in Ozeanien*. Göttingen 1959

Sébillot, Paul, *Légendes, croyances et superstitions de la mer*. Paris 1886–1887

–, *Le folklore des pêcheurs*. Paris 1901

Seligman, Charles Gabriel, *Melanesians of British New Guinea*. Cambridge 1910

Sopher, David E., *The sea nomads*. Singapore 1965

Spamer, Adolf, *Die Tätowierung in den deutschen Hafenstädten*. Niederdeutsche Zeitschrift für Volkskunde 11 (1933)

Spies, M.H., *Veteran steamers*. Humlebaek 1965

Stackpole, Edouard A., *Scrimshaw at Mystic Seaport*. Mystic Connect. 1958

Steinmann, Alfred, *Das kultische Schiff in Indonesien*. Ipek 13/14 (1939/40)

Stephan, Bruno, *Märkische Schifferdörfer*. Brandenburgia 37 (1928)

Suder, Hans, *Vom Einbaum und Floß zum Schiff*. Berlin 1930

Szymanski, Hans, *Der Ever der Niederelbe*. Lübeck 1932

–, *Deutsche Segelschiffe*. Berlin 1934

–, *Schiffsmodelle in niedersächsischen Kirchen*. Göttingen 1966

Theel, Gustav Adolf, *Der seefahrende Mensch und seine Probleme. Gesellschaft in Geschichte und Gegenwart*. Berlin (West) 1961

Timm, Werner, *Kapitänsbilder. Schiffsporträts seit 1782*. Rostock 1971

Ucelli, Guido, *Le navi di Nemi*. Rome 1940

Vilkuna, Kustaa, *Formen und Organisation einer alten saisonmäßigen Fischersiedlung an der Küste des Bottnischen Meerbusens*. Kolloquium Balticum Ethnographicum 1966. Berlin 1968

Vogel, Walther, *Die Namen der Schiffe im Spiegel von Volks- und Zeitcharakter*. Berlin 1912

Vogel, Walther, *Geschichte der deutschen Seeschiffahrt*. Berlin 1915

Wachsmuth, Dietrich, *Untersuchungen zu den antiken Sakralhandlungen bei Seereisen*. Phil. Diss. Berlin (West) 1967

Ward, Barbara, *Floating villages – Chinese fishermen in Hong Kong*. Man 59 (1959)

Waters, David W., *The art of navigation in England in Elizabethan and early Stuart times*. London 1958

Webb, W.J. & Robert W.Carrick, *The pictorial history of outboard motors*. New York 1967

Weibust, Knut, *Deep sea sailors – A study in maritime ethnology*. Stockholm 1969

Willis, Fred C., *Die niederländische Marinemalerei*. Leipzig 1911

White, Walter, *Sea gypsies of Malaya*. London 1922

Winter, Heinrich, *Die Kolumbusschiffe*. Burg 1944, Rostock 1960, 2nd ed.

–, *Die Katalanische Nao von 1450*. Burg 1956

–, *Das Hanseschiff im ausgehenden 15. Jahrhundert*. Rostock 1961

Winter, Marie Luise, *Bänkellieder vom Untergang der "Cimbria" und "Austria"*. Niederdeutsche Zeitschrift für Volkskunde 20 (1942)

Worcester, George R.G., *Junks and sampans of the Yangtze*. Vol. 1–2. Shanghai 1947 to 1948

Wossidlo, Richard, *Reise, Quartier, in Gottesnaam. Das Seemannsleben im Munde alter Fahrensleute*. Rostock 1940–1943

Wright, E.V. & C.W.Wright, *The North Ferriby boats*. Mariner's Mirror 33 (1947), 50 (1964)

Zechlin, Egmont, *Maritime Weltgeschichte*. Hamburg 1947

Adze a tool used in shipwrighting for shaping wooden parts by chip removal. It has a steel blade at right angles to the shaft, the cutting edge of which may be ground on one or both sides, or hollow ground; the effect is produced by an angled chopping motion and acts on plane surfaces and edges

Aft behind; after end of vessel

Ballast any weight not part of a regular cargo or stores, carried by a vessel in order to safeguard stability (sand, stones, iron bars, water, etc.)

Bark, barque sailing vessel of three, four or five masts, square-rigged on all but the aftermost mast, which carries fore-and-aft sails only

Beacon any fixed structure (often combined with a light) to mark a channel or hazard

Belay to make fast (of a rope)

Blade the broad end of an oar or paddle

Block pulley in its housing

Block stem (or stern) a main structural detail of boat end types: the stem (or stern) is shaped with the axe or adze out of a section of a tree log which may be full round or split in half

Board originally the side of the ship's hull, or edge of the deck; now applied to the entirety of the vessel, e.g. "on board". Also, the sides or legs of a zig-zag course such as that made when going to windward

Boom spar at the foot of a sail; light spars run out at the end of spars; poles run out at the bow and stern of fishing vessels for the attachment of lines guiding the submerged purse seine while fishing

Bottom plank a main structural element of boat bottom types: a heavy plank formed by longitudinally sawn and joined timber, laid down on the broad or flat side

Bottom shell a main structural element of boat bottom types: a shell formed by the hollowing of a log section, which may be round or split in half

Brace ropes attached to the two ends of a yard, for the horizontal adjustment (bracing) of the yard

Brig a two-masted vessel, square-rigged on both masts

Bulkhead on shore: a system of shore protection, consisting of posts driven into the ground supporting layers of horizontal beams, which are braced by an infill of stones and earth between the wall formed by the beams and the shore; in vessels: transverse partition built of planks, iron or steel, solidly fastened to the sides, forming separate compartments

Buoy floating, anchored navigational mark, designating a channel or hazard

Capstan a winch with vertical axle

Carvel laid (or built) a method of direct (shell method) or indirect (frame method) joining of the side planks of a vessel's hull, resulting in a smooth (flush) outer skin

Centerboard a vertically movable device used to increase the immersed surface of a vessel's hull, thus diminishing sideways drift; also used as a steering aid, especially on rafts. Several types exist: longitudinally penetrating the bottom (sliding keel, centerboard, dagger board); suspended over the side (leeboard) and hoisted above water level when not in use

Cleat nautical: a wooden or metal device for the fastening (belaying) of ropes; a strip of wood nailed to a surface, e.g. for the support of shelving, or to provide a foothold on a gangplank, etc. a clamp

Clinker built or lapstrake a method of direct joining of side planks, by means of sewing (lacing), spiking or riveting; resulting in a stepwise overlapping of planks (Ill. 16)

Close-hauled a vessel "going to windward" is said to be sailing close-hauled. When a specific point in the windward direction is to be reached (e.g. a harbor entrance), requiring more or less frequent "going about" or "tacking", the term "beating to windward" is used

Compass card a round, freely rotating disk connected with the magnetic compass, divided formerly in "points" (thirty-two in number, each of 11.25°) nowadays in degrees

Crabclaw sail collective designation for various forms of fore-and-aft sails in use in Oceania. They are triangular, spread by two spars diverging on a plane, and have a fixed tack; they may be set asymmetrically either at one or the other side of the mast, or unilaterally abaft the mast (Ill. 28 h)

Derrick mast a mast formed by two spars facing each other (bipod) on a line perpendicular to the keel, or by three spars arranged on a triangular plan (tripod); in either case, inclined toward one another and lashed together at the top

Dip saluting, by means of lowering and hoisting the flag of a vessel in rapid succession; to depress a yard by hauling down the windward end

Dock an enclosed area of water, the level of which may be regulated by means of gates; used either as a harbor basin, or in shipyards for constructing and repairing hulls

Dowelling the method of joining planks together by means of hardwood pegs (dowels, also called treenails or trunnels) driven into auger holes (Ill. 16)

Drift the motion of a vessel through the water other than by human control, i.e. through currents, tidal streams, wind action, etc.

Fish trap a stationary fishing device operated without supervision, made of basket material or of nets, constructed on the principle of the labyrinth

Fore-and-aft sails sails which are rigged, when not in use, in a parallel position to the keel. They are much more effective in going to windward than squaresails

Forecastle the foremost part of the ship's deck, which formerly also housed the crew

Foremast the mast nearest to the bow, with the exception of those rigs in which the second mast is shorter than the first. The term is used only for rigs of two or more masts

Frame one of the many transverse ribs of a ship's framework. Originally made of naturally bent or grown wood in a single piece on each side of the hull; in the later more differentiated technique built up of sawn pieces, consisting of a bottom timber (the floor) and two or more side pieces (the futtocks)

Frame construction technique of shipbuilding, with the following sequence: laying the keel; erection of stem and stern post and frames (ribs); covering the framework with its skin, i.e. planking

Full-rigged ship a sailing ship of three or more masts with square rig on all masts

Gaff a spar with a claw-shaped fork at the throat (the end next to the mast), used to hold the sail out from the mast

Gaff sail quadrilateral sail, spread at the head by a gaff; set abaft the mast, with the leading edge (luff) fastened to the mast (Ill. 28g)

Galeas two-masted vessel, with the mainmast in front and mizzenmast behind

Galley cook house on deck; a ship's kitchen

Gunwale the upper edge of the side planking

Half-hourglass old-fashioned nautical sand clock timed to run out in thirty minutes. Each

turning over of the clock was marked by the stroke of a bell – one "glas" (German) or one bell

Halyard ropes (and tackle) for raising and lowering of spars (yards and gaffs) and sails

Hatchway deck opening, bordered by a coaming (upstand) and closed by a hatch cover

Hawse strongly reinforced and lined hole through the hull, above the waterline in the bow, for the passage of the anchor chain or hawser

Heave to raise a weight; to shorten the hauling part of a purchase in the direction opposite to the load (heave in); also used in connection with operating the capstan, winch and pumps

Helm tiller, or any other mechanism to control the lateral movement of the rudder

Inside stem or stern a main structural detail of boat end types: a stem or stern made of longitudinally joined sections sawn from larger timbers, and covered by the ends of the side planking, the stem (or stern) thus being invisible from the outside

Jib triangular fore-and-aft sail, set between the foremost mast and the bow or bowsprit or jib-boom, usually from a stay. A jib set "flying" is not attached to a stay

Junk sail quadrilateral fore-and-aft sail, spread by a yard at the head and a boom at the foot as well as by a number of battens across the sail at angles progressively increasing above the horizontal, counting upwards; suspended asymmetrically on either side of the mast, with a loose luff and freely pivoting tack (Ill. 28e)

Keel the backbone of the vessel; a timber hewn out of a full or half log; if laid flat called a bottom keel, if laid vertically, a timber keel

Knot unit of speed per hour; one knot equals one sea mile (6080 feet) per hour. No longer used as a unit of distance

Lash to fasten tightly, usually by tying down with rope, chain, etc.

Lateen sail triangular or quadrangular fore-and-aft sail, set and lowered with a sloping yard attached to the head on either side of the mast; loose-footed and, if quadrangular, with a loose luff; the tack is fastened at the bow (Ill. 28f)

Launching putting a vessel into the water; specifically, the act and ceremony of first committing a newly built vessel to the water, normally combined with naming her

Lee, leeward the side or direction opposite to the wind direction

Leech designates the side opposed to the "luff" or forward edge of a sail, although squaresails are said to have two leeches. Derived from "lee edge"

Log the ship's journal; a nautical device for measuring the speed of a vessel through the water

Lugsail quadrangular fore-and-aft sail, set and lowered with a sloping yard (the lug) spreading the head at either side of the mast. Lugsails may be loose-footed; with the tack fastened to the mast (standing lug) or to the bow or deck (dipping lug); a third type, fitted with a boom at the foot, has the tack freely pivoting (balance lug) (Ill. 28 c, d)

Mainmast in vessels with two or more masts, the second mast from the bow, with the exception of the galeas, ketch and yawl on which the second, after mast is the shorter

Mast pillars a system of vertically joined timbers extending from the ship's bottom to the deck beams, to support the mast and assist in its lateral bracing

Mast step a wooden block seated on top of the keel, with a hollow space to receive the heel of the mast

Marlinspike a thorn-shaped rigger's tool used in splicing; made of steel or wood, it is thrust between the strands of a rope

Mile the geographical or nautical mile has 6080 feet; the statute or land mile, 5280 feet

Mizzenmast in three-masted vessels, the aftermost mast; the only two-masted rigs with a mizzenmast are the galeas, ketch and yawl, in which the after mast is shorter

Mould loft a large loft within the shipyard, on the floor of which the cross sections of the vessel to be built are drawn in their actual dimensions for making moulds, from which the frames and other timbers are shaped

Oilskins workclothes for bad weather, formerly made of canvas saturated in linseed oil

Outrigger any lateral extensions of the width of a vessel above the water surface; specifically, oar rests with oarlocks or thole pins projecting sideways from the gunwale and beyond the side

Parrel device for holding a yard or the throat of a gaff to the mast, permitting vertical movement as well as pivoting; often a bent wooden or iron hoop, also a length of rope strung with wooden beads to reduce friction on the mast

Pay out to lengthen or let out the hauling part of a purchase in the direction of the load; in the case of the sheet (of a sail) it is "eased"

Point old-fashioned division of the nautical compass card of 1/32 of a circle, or 11.25°; describes the angle the ship's keel makes with the wind direction, when sailing to windward, e.g. to point 60° off the wind

Port (side) designates the left side of the vessel, looking forward

Port hole a window, usually circular, in the side of a vessel, heavily glazed, which can be opened and closed

Rig designates the type of sailing vessel in terms of sail plan, e.g. brig rig, barque rig, etc.

Rigging the ropes and wires used to brace the spars and adjust and control sails. Standing rigging (shrouds, stays, backstays) is fixed and supports the masts; running rigging (halyards, sheets, braces, lifts, downhauls, clewlines, buntlines, etc.) is manipulated as necessary in sailing. As a verb, the term is also used to mean making a temporary arrangement, e.g. rigging a Spanish burton, rigging a head pump, etc.

Schooner vessel of two or more masts, with fore-and-aft rig (traditionally gaff rig). The main, taller mast is aft, with a shorter foremast

Sculling propulsion by means of a single oar, which is streamed out behind over the stern and moved back and forth in short sidewise strokes, the wrist imparting to the oar a helix-like semi-rotation and counter-rotation with each stroke

Set, setting of sails. The term has several uses, such as adding more sails to those already employed, or: the ship set (i.e. was able to set) skysails on all three masts, etc. Also refers to the position of any sail while working to best advantage as opposed to the resting position, or the position it occupies when furled

Sextant navigator's instrument for measuring angles the basic frame of which has the shape of a sixth of a circle, i.e. a 60° arc.

Sheer the curvature of the deck line fore and aft, as seen in profile

Sheet rope or tackle for the adjustment of the lower and after part of a fore-and-aft sail, or of the leeward lower corner of a square fore-sail or mainsail (the windward one being held by the tack tackle), or of the two lower corners of any other squaresail

Shell construction pre-industrial shipbuilding technique, with the following stages: laying the keel or bottom plank; erecting stem and stern post; planking the sides; inserting interior timbers (knees, braces, etc.)

Shroud part of the standing rigging: lateral supporting ropes or wires leading from the mast or masthead to the ship's sides, or from the head of an upper mast to the sides of the platform (the "top") of a lower mast, e.g. topmast or topgallant shrouds

Skylight hatchways with hinged, glazed covers, for the admission of light and air to cabins or engine room

Sounding ascertaining the depth of water by means of the lead line

Spiking the method of joining planks together by means of wrought iron nails of square section; they are driven obliquely through both planks above and below the seam, with countersunk heads (Ill. 16)

Splicing joining rope without knots, by interweaving the separated strands of one end with the loosened strands of the other

Spritsail a quadrangular or (rarely) triangular fore-and-aft sail, with the luff and tack fastened to the mast, and spread by means of one or (rarely) two poles or spars diagonally across the sail; the entire sail area is abaft the mast

Square rig simple square rig: a single squaresail set from a one-piece mast; differentiated square rig: originally the sail area on each mast was divided in two, later three, sails set on a two-part mast; later, with the subdivision of topsails and topgallantsails and the addition of royals and occasionally skysails, the rig consisted of from four to seven sails, set on a three-part mast (Ill. 28a, b)

Squaresail quadrangular sail, set from and furled to a yard, at right angles to the keel in the resting position; when sailing, extended symmetrically on either side of the mast (Ill. 28)

Starboard the right side of the vessel, looking forward

Stay part of the standing rigging: a supporting rope or wire extending from the mast or masthead parallel to the keel, to the bow or stern

Steering generally, vessels are steered from the after end (rarely from both ends) and a variety of mechanisms are in use; a distinction can be made between steering oar and rudder; the former is suspended either from one side (starboard) of the upper side planks or from both sides; the latter is centrally attached at the sternpost on the keel axis

Stem main structural element of front ends of boats and ships, occurring in various forms, such as timber stem, block stem, thwartships stem or inside stem

Stemhead assembly a configuration of several timbers (knightheads, cutwater, trail boards) jointly supporting the bowsprit

Stern the after (back) part of the vessel; specifically, the main structural element of boat end types, analogous in construction to the stem. The shape of the stern also forms a main characteristic; the principal types are pointed, round or square (as seen in plan view)

Sternpost heavy timber closing the hull aft, and serving as support for the rudder. In pre-industrialized building the sternpost is apt to show the same characteristics as distinguish the stem of the various types

Superstructure deckhouse and other enclosed spaces erected on deck

Tack the forward lower corner of fore-and-aft sails; whichever of the two lower corners of a squaresail is nearer the bow

Tacking a sailing manœuvre: altering course when going to windward, by turning the ship's head into the wind (luffing) until the wind is from directly ahead; continuing to turn, the ship "goes about" until she "fills" on the other tack

Tackle any system of pulleys comprising a minimum of two sheaves or blocks

Taking bearings the method of determining the vessel's position by compass bearings of land or sea marks

Tarpaulin tarred or oiled canvas, used in covers for protecting hatchways, lifeboats, etc. In older times, sailors made heavy weather hats for themselves out of this material

Thole pins wooden pegs projecting upward from the gunwale: the space between acts as a bearing for the pivoting oar

Thwart a lateral boat timber or plank, fitted horizontally between the upper plank strakes at right angles to the keel; commonly used as a boat seat

Thwartships stem a timber joined to the hull sides with its broad side at right angles to the keel

Timbers lateral or longitudinal structural parts of a ship's frame; also, interior strengthening pieces, e.g. knees, braces, stringers, floors, etc.

Timber stem (or stern) longitudinally joined timber sections sawn out of larger pieces

Top the upper extremity of a pole mast, especially the section above the fids, or rests for the standing rigging; on a full-rigged (three-part) mast, the platform at the top of the lower mast, which serves as a strut or spreader for the topmast shrouds

Topgallant the topmost, or third, part of a full-rigged mast. In the older differentiated square rig, the topgallant sail was the third from the bottom; subsequent to the topsails

being divided into upper and lower topsails, the topgallant sails were similarly divided. Where in use, royals and skysails were also set from the topgallant mast

Top hamper refers to the entire rigging of a vessel (spars, ropes and sails), especially those parts above the lower masts

Topsail in the older differentiated square rig, the second squaresail from the bottom; later divided into lower and upper topsails. In fore-and-aft rigs, triangular or square fore-and-aft sails set above gaff sails, sometimes referred to as gaff topsails, are still in use. Topsails were also used over lug rigs and even with the lateen rig

Transom horizontally laid closing planks and supporting timbers forming square sterns

Trim to adjust the cargo, the ballast, or both, so as to assure the optimal position of the ship's hull in the water

Upper masts extensions of the lower mast, normally fitted so as to permit lowering (housing). The spar above the lower mast is the topmast in both fore-and-aft and square rig. The latter normally comprises a topgallant mast set above the topmast

Wearing altering course by turning the ship's head away from the wind, then swinging onto the new course

Wind vane a small, triangular flag, or a long, narrow, tapering cloth tube spread open at one end by a ring, at the mast truck, to indicate wind direction

Windward the side or direction facing the wind

Yard a spar for spreading the head of a sail, most commonly a squaresail, but also used on lugsails, lateen sails, studding sails, etc.

Picture Sources

Ålands Sjofartsmuseum, Mariehamn: 96. Archive: 101, 163. Arktisk Institut, Charlottenlund: 11. Lala Aufsberg, Sonthofen: 35, 87, 148. Bruno Barbey/Magnum, Paris: 9. Bavaria-Verlag/Gardi, Gauting near Munich: 152. Beken of Cowes, Marine Photographers: 160. Hugo Bernatzik, Vienna: 29. Bibliothèque Nationale, Paris: 85, 138. Blekinge Museum, Karlskrona: 108. British Museum, London: 14. Centro de Estudos de Etnologia, Lisbon: 3. Arne Emil Christensen, Oslo: 113. Detroit Institute of Arts, Detroit: 106. Deutsche Staatsbibliothek/Richter, Berlin: 1, 22, 30, 59, 74, 76, 77, 78, 80, 116, 134. Deutsches Archäologisches Institut, Bagdad: 143. Günter Ewald, Stralsund: 70. T. L. Feininger, Cambridge/Mass.: 112. J. t'Felt/Jules van Beylen, Antwerp: 21. Focke-Museum, Bremen: 69. Frobenius-Institut für Völkerkunde, Frankfort on the Main: 24, 52 (Haberland). René Gardi, Bern: 47, 153, 154. Handels- og Søfartsmuseet Kronborg, Helsingør: 111, 131, 133, 135, 142. Claus Hansmann, Munich: 23, 64, 72, 155. Olof Hasslöf, Malmö: 38. Henning Henningsen, Helsingør: 97, 103. Holle-Bildarchiv, Baden-Baden: 45. Hürlimann/Atlantis-Verlag, Zurich: 49. Institute for Seatraining, Tokio: 99. Institut für vergleichende Verhaltensforschung der Österr. Akademie der Wissenschaften/Koenig, Vienna: 123. Institut für Theaterwissenschaft, Universität Köln, Sammlung Niessen, Cologne: 110. Stig Tio Karlsson, Vaxholm: 125, 161. Dr. H. E. Kauffmann, Munich: 19. Kgl. Vitterhedsakademien, Stockholm: 66. Dr. Kühlmann, Berlin: 117. Kulturhistorisches Museum, Stralsund: 68. Eugen Kusch, Schwarzenbruck near Nuremberg: 4, 12, 58, 144. Laenderpress, Düsseldorf-Golzheim: 10, 50, 149, 157. Larry Le Sage, Ottawa: 26. Mariners Museum, Newport News (Va.): 100, 132. Maritiem Museum "Prins Hendrik", Rotterdam: 71. Middet-Foto, Oslo: 65. Museo d'Antichità, Ravenna: 37. Museo Navale Romano, Albenga: 39. Museo Storico Navale, Venice: 89, 119. Museum für Völkerkunde, Basel: 57. Museum für Völkerkunde, Leipzig: p.83. National Maritime Museum, London-Greenwich: 107. National Scheepvaartsmuseum, Antwerp: 63. Norsk Folkemuseum, Oslo: 146. Outboard Marine International Inc., Miami: 156. Peabody Museum of Salem (Mass.): 91, 94, 98. Peesch, Berlin: 150. Popper Ltd., London: 51, 151. Pressens Bild AB, Stockholm: 33. Prillinger, Gmunden (Upper Austria): 120. Rijksmuseum, Amsterdam: 83. Gerhard Reinhold, Mölkau near Leipzig: 88, 141. Wolfgang Rudolph, Schildow: 114, 124, 145. Schleswig-Holsteinisches Landesmuseum, Schleswig: 127. Staatliche Museen zu Berlin, Berlin: 34, 36, 40, 93, 95, 126, 129, 130. Statens Museum för Kunst, Copenhagen: 121. Statens Sjöhistoriska Museum, Stockholm: 84. Miloslaw Stingl, Prague: 128. Sonnfried Streicher, Stralsund: 8. Herbert Strobel, Leipzig: 6, 13, 18, 27, 158. The New York Historical Society, New York: 109. Victoria & Albert Museum, London: 44. Vikingeskibshallen Roskilde: 67, p.221. Walter Verlag AG, Olten: 54. Hein Wenzel, Berlin: 159. Michael Wolgensinger, Zurich: 122. Zaamlandse Oudheidkamer, Zaandijk: 89. Zentralbibliothek Zurich: 75. Zentrale Farbbildagentur, Düsseldorf: 5, 25, 46, 55, 56, 118 and motif on jacket.